The Next Room of the Dream

As with a dream interpreted by one still sleeping,
The interpretation is only the next room of the dream.
   —"To Clio, Muse of History," page 3

poems and two plays

THE
NEXT
ROOM
OF
THE
DREAM

by *HOWARD NEMEROV* *published by The University of Chicago Press*

Acknowledgment is made to the editors of the
periodicals in which the poems first appeared—
The Carleton Miscellany, The Dubliner, Harper's,
The Hudson Review, The Nation,
The New Yorker, The New York Times,
The Noble Savage, The Northwestern Tri-Quarterly,
The Outsider, Partisan Review, Poetry,
Poetry Dial, The Reporter, The Saturday Evening Post,
The Shasta Review, The London Times Literary Supplement,
Western Poetry Review.

THE UNIVERSITY OF CHICAGO PRESS, CHICAGO & LONDON
The University of Toronto Press, Toronto 5, Canada

TO *Kay Boyle*

Contents

I Effigies

To Clio, Muse of History

*On learning that The Etruscan Warrior
in the Metropolitan Museum of Art
is proved a modern forgery*

One more casualty,
One more screen memory penetrated at last
To be destroyed in the endless anamnesis
Always progressing, never arriving at a cure.
My childhood in the glare of that giant form
Corrupts with history, for I too fought in the War.

He, great male beauty
That stood for the sexual thrust of power,
His target eyes inviting the universal victim
To fatal seduction, the crested and greaved
Survivor long after shield and sword are dust,
Has now become another lie about our life.

Smash the idol, of course.
Bury the pieces deep as the interest of truth
Requires. And you may in time compose the future
Smoothly without him, though it is too late
To disinfect the past of his huge effigy
By any further imposition of your hands.

But tell us no more
Enchantments, Clio. History has given
And taken away; murders become memories,
And memories become the beautiful obligations:
As with a dream interpreted by one still sleeping,
The interpretation is only the next room of the dream.

For I remember how
We children stared, learning from him
Unspeakable things about war that weren't in the books;
And how the Museum store offered for sale
His photographic reproductions in full color
With the ancient genitals blacked out.

Santa Claus

Somewhere on his travels the strange Child
Picked up with this overstuffed confidence man,
Affection's inverted thief, who climbs at night
Down chimneys, into dreams, with this world's goods.
Bringing all the benevolence of money,
He teaches the innocent to want, thus keeps
Our fat world rolling. His prescribed costume,
White flannel beard, red belly of cotton waste,
Conceals the thinness of essential hunger,
An appetite that feeds on satisfaction;
Or, pregnant with possessions, he brings forth
Vanity and the void. His name itself
Is corrupted, and even Saint Nicholas, in his turn,
Gives off a faint and reminiscent stench,
The merest soupçon, of brimstone and the pit.

Now, at the season when the Child is born
To suffer for the world, suffer the world,
His bloated Other, jovial satellite
And sycophant, makes his appearance also
In a glitter of goodies, in a rock candy glare.
Played at the better stores by bums, for money,
This annual savior of the economy
Speaks in the parables of the dollar sign:
Suffer the little children to come to Him.

At Easter, he's anonymous again,
Just one of the crowd lunching on Calvary.

To the Mannequins

Adorable images,
Plaster of Paris
Lilies of the field,
You are not alive, therefore
Pathos will be out of place.

But I have learned
A fact about your fate,
And it is this:

After you go out of fashion
Beneath your many fashions,
Or when your elbows and knees
Have been bruised powdery white,
So that you are no good to anybody—

They will take away your gowns,
Your sables and bathing suits,
Leaving exposed before all men
Your inaccessible bellies
And pointless nubilities.

Movers will come by night
And load you into trucks
And take you away to the Camps,
Where soldiers, or the State Police,
Will use you as targets
For small-arms practice,

Leading me to inquire,
Since pathos is out of place,
What it is that they are practicing.

Fontenelle

At night, passing the open door
Of the power station, you look inside
At an immense, immaculate, lofty space
Of marble floors and green iron grille work
Climbing on windows cathedrally tall.

The shields of their backs showing as giant humps,
The dynamos gleam deep in their own light.
They have been sunk partly into the floor
And set apart behind railings, as man sets apart
Whatever he would find famous and disturbing:
The way the great globe is in the Daily News
Building, or Grant is in Grant's Tomb.

An old man in a grey sweater sits by the door,
The night watchman, reading a comic book.
Sometimes he stops to spit on the floor,
And after the comic book he has an obscene
Magazine. It is a long night
In the power plant.

Fontenelle wrote these books among others:
The *Apologie des Tourbillons*, the *Dialogues des Morts*,
The *Entretiens sur la Pluralité des Mondes*.
He lived to be one hundred years old.

The dynamos, deep sunken in their own light,
Hum to themselves. Not of the dragon's wake,
The moonlit rinsings of the China Sea,
Not of the wind in the furnace of the North.
They are of the type called "self-exciting."

Someone asked Fontenelle, Did he never laugh?
Non non, monsieur, je ne fais jamais ah-ah-ah.
And when he got to be a hundred years old,
Somebody asked him what he felt about being
    a hundred years old.
Rien, seulement une certaine difficulté d'être.

The Iron Characters

The iron characters, keepers of the public confidence,
The sponsors, fund raisers, and members of the board,
Who naturally assume their seats among the governors,
Who place their names behind the issue of bonds
And are consulted in the formation of cabinets,
The catastrophes of war, depression, and natural disaster:
They represent us in responsibilities many and great.
It is no wonder, then, if in a moment of crisis,
Before the microphones, under the lights, on a great occasion,
One of them will break down in hysterical weeping
Or fall in an epileptic seizure, or if one day
We read in the papers of one's having been found
Naked and drunk in a basement with three high school boys,
Of one who jumped from the window of his hospital room.
For are they not as ourselves in these things also?
Let the orphan, the pauper, the thief, the derelict drunk
And all those of no fixed address, shed tears of rejoicing
For the broken minds of the strong, the torn flesh of the just.

Don Juan to the Statue

Dominant marble, neither will I yield!
The soul endures at one with its election,
Lover to bed or soldier to the field,
Your daughter's the cause of this & that erection.

Journey of the Snowmen

Gradually in gardens
The cold men melted,
Becoming featureless
As powerful Pharaohs
Slumped in the long sleep.
That's how things were
In the Old Kingdom.

Now, by a miracle
Reborn, they assemble
Under the influence
Of light, they crowd
At the highest corners
To testify in a babble
Of tongues that they are going
To glitter in the gutters
And snakedance down all hills
And hollows, on the long fall
That makes the sewers sing.

The Daily Globe

Each day another installment of the old
Romance of Order brings to the breakfast table
The paper flowers of catastrophe.
One has this recurrent dream about the world.

Headlines declare the ambiguous oracles,
The comfortable old prophets mutter doom.
Man's greatest intellectual pleasure is
To repeat himself, yet somehow the daily globe

Rolls on, while the characters in comic strips
Prolong their slow, interminable lives
Beyond the segregated photographs
Of the girls that marry and the men that die.

A Picture

Of people running down the street
Among the cars, a good many people.
You could see that something was up,
Because people in American towns
Don't ordinarily run, they walk,
And not in the street. The camera caught
A pretty girl tilted off-balance
And with her mouth in O amazed;
A man in a fat white shirt, his tie
Streaming behind him, as one flat foot
Went slap on the asphalt—you could see
He was out of breath, but dutifully
Running along with all the others,
Maybe at midday, on Main Street somewhere.

The running faces did not record
Hatred or anger or great enthusiasm
For what they were doing (hunting down
A Negro, according to the caption),
But seemed rather solemn, intent,
With the serious patience of animals
Driven through a gate by some
Urgency out of the camera's range,
On an occasion too serious
For private feeling. The breathless faces
Expressed a religion of running,
A form of ritual exaltation
Devoted to obedience, and
Obedient, it might be, to the Negro,
Who was not caught by the camera
When it took the people in the street
Among the cars, toward some object,
Seriously running.

Nothing Will Yield

Nothing will yield. The pretty poems are dead,
And the mad poets in their periwigs,
Bemused upon a frontispiece before
The ruined Temple of Art, and supervised
By the Goddess of Reason leaning from a cloud,
In reality died insane. Alas, for the grave
And gaudy forms! Lord Hi and Lady Ho,
Those brazen effigies upon a plinth
Of pink granite, seem immutable,
But seem. In time, they have many tongues,
But in eternity Latin is spoken.

Or else, perhaps, it is all a matter of hats,
The helmet, the biretta, the iron crown,
The crown of thorns. Lachrymae Christi is
A beautiful sound, a Neapolitan wine,
The Tears of Christ. And yet nothing will yield.
How many are the uniforms of time
That men and women wear, how grave the glitter
Of epaulets and emblems as the grand
Procession passes, how nobly they speak
The language of the court, the holy language
That scorns the isolation of the heart.
It takes great courage to go on the stage.

One Forever Alien

When I become the land, when they will build
Blast furnaces over me, and lay black asphalt
For hundreds of miles across my ribs, and wheels
Begin to bounce interminably on the bone;
When I enter, at last, America, when I am
Part of her progress and a true patriot,
And the schoolchildren sing of my sacrifice,
Remembering the burial day of my birth—
Then even the efficient will have to forgive me,
The investigators approve my security,
And those that harden their hearts welcome me home.

Then, in that day, my countrymen,
When I shall come among you fleeced as the lamb
And in the diaper of the grave newly arrayed,
The Adam Qadmon, the greenhorn immigrant,
Shall pass the customs at the port of entry
Where the Guardian Lady lifts her flaming sword.
Forgiven the original sin of his origin,
He comes as a bond redeemed, as newly negotiable,
    To be as a soybean before you.

A Predecessor of Perseus

Since he is older than Hamlet or Stavrogin,
Older than Leopold Bloom; since he has been
Stravaging through the Dark Wood several years
Beyond the appointed time, meeting no wolf,
Leopard, or lion, not to mention Virgil;
And long since seen the span of Keats conclude,
And the span of Alexander,—he begins
At last to wonder.

           Had his sacred books
Misled him? Or had he deceived himself?
Like some he knew, who'd foolishly confused
The being called and being chosen; they
Ran down the crazy pavement of their path
On primrose all the way.

              An old friend said,
"The first thing to learn about wisdom is
This, that you can't do anything with it."
Wisdom. If that was what he had, he might,
Like a retired witch, keep it locked up
In the broom closet. But he rides his road,
Passing the skinless elder skeletons
Who smile, and maybe he will keep on going
Until the grey unbearable she of the world
Shall raise her eyes, and recognize, and grin
At her eternal amateur's approach,
All guts no glass, to meet her gaze head on
And be stricken in the likeness of himself
At least, if not of Keats or Alexander.

II *Emblems*

A Spell before Winter

After the red leaf and the gold have gone,
Brought down by the wind, then by hammering rain
Bruised and discolored, when October's flame
Goes blue to guttering in the cusp, this land
Sinks deeper into silence, darker into shade.
There is a knowledge in the look of things,
The old hills hunch before the north wind blows.

Now I can see certain simplicities
In the darkening rust and tarnish of the time,
And say over the certain simplicities,
The running water and the standing stone,
The yellow haze of the willow and the black
Smoke of the elm, the silver, silent light
Where suddenly, readying toward nightfall,
The sumac's candelabrum darkly flames.
And I speak to you now with the land's voice,
It is the cold, wild land that says to you
A knowledge glimmers in the sleep of things:
The old hills hunch before the north wind blows.

Human Things

When the sun gets low, in winter,
The lapstreaked side of a red barn
Can put so flat a stop to its light
You'd think everything was finished.

Each dent, fray, scratch, or splinter,
Any gray weathering where the paint
Has scaled off, is a healed scar
Grown harder with the wounds of light.

Only a tree's trembling shadow
Crosses that ruined composure; even
Nail holes look deep enough to swallow
Whatever light has left to give.

And after sundown, when the wall
Slowly surrenders its color, the rest
Remains, its high, obstinate
Hulk more shadowy than the night.

Winter Exercise

A man out walking alone in the snow,
Painfully cold, blinded by wind and snow,
And with nowhere in particular to go
But round in a circle, over the wooded hill
And down, back round by the road and past the mill
And up street again to his own doorsill—
Now what may such a man be but a lost
Man, aimlessly battling the snowy host
To get nowhere but home, where his own ghost
Will meet him, bowing, on the parlor floor,
Join him again when he's scarce through the door,
Enjoin him against wandering any more?

Suppose, instead, he really did get lost
There on the hill, beyond surveyor's post
And sidewalk, and Bohemia grew a coast
Which loomed before him, white as the white storm
Blowing into his eyes? With what good form
Would things be kept up by his ghost at the warm
Hearthside at home: His slippers and his drink,
No dust on the floor, or dishes in the sink;
It might be days till anyone would think
There was a kind of stillness to all this
Which made the house, though cheerful, an abyss,
And unidentifiably remiss.

Meanwhile his seven-league, left-handed heart
Had kept him circling up there, far apart
From what his ghost, out of domestic art,
Could manage in the way of keeping life
Respectable and decent (keep his wife
From noticing, for instance). His hard strife
Against the storm had long begun to seem

Unduly long, a walk around a dream
Whose nonsense only waking could redeem;
Till, seeing everywhere nothing but deep
Snow and dark woods, he knew he was asleep,
And, to wake up, lay down and went to sleep.

He dreamed a warm, familiar dream of home,
Went, like an auctioneer, from room to room.
Table and chair, razor and brush and comb
He catalogued, and the lady too whose lord
He was, who shared his castle, bed and board,
And realized in his dream that he was bored.
"There's nothing in this for me," he said aloud;
"Better the snow should be my lonely shroud."
The ghost at home heard, looked around, allowed
The force of this, and followed: Up the hill
He went, through snow, across the same doorsill
Stepped into dream; and soon the lady will.

Idea

Idea blazes in darkness, a lonely star.
The witching hour is not twelve, but one.
Pure thought, in principle, some say, is near
Madness, but the independent mind thinks on,
Breathing and burning, abstract as the air.

Supposing all this were a game of chess.
One learned to do without the pieces first,
And then the board; and finally, I guess,
Without the game. The lightship gone adrift,
Endangering others with its own distress.

O holy light! All other stars are gone,
The shapeless constellations sag and fall
Till navigation fails, though ships go on
This merry, mad adventure as before
Their single-minded masters meant to drown.

Somewhere

A girl this evening regrets her surrender with tears,
A schoolboy knows he will be unprepared tomorrow.
A father, aware of having behaved viciously,
Is unable to speak; his child weeps obstinately.
Somewhere a glutton waits for himself to vomit,
An unfaithful wife resists the temptation to die.

The stones of the city have been here for centuries,
The tides have been washing backwards and forwards
In sunlight, in starlight, since before the beginning.
Down in the swamp a red fox runs quietly, quietly
Under the owl's observation, those yellow eyes
That eat through the darkness. Hear the shrew cry!

Somewhere a story is told, someone is singing
Of careless love in the hands of its creditors.
It is of Yseult, Antigone, Tarquin with Lucrece,
The Brides in the Bath. . . . Those who listen
Lean forward bemused, rapt with the sweet seductions
Punishable by death, with the song's word: long ago.

De Anima

Now it is night, now in the brilliant room
A girl stands at the window looking out,
But sees, in the darkness of the frame,
Only her own image.

And there is a young man across the street
Who looks at the girl and into the brilliant room.
They might be in love, might be about to meet,
If this were a romance.

In looking at herself, she tries to look
Beyond herself, and half become another,
Admiring and resenting, maybe dreaming
Her lover might see her so.

The other, the stranger standing in cold and dark,
Looks at the young girl in her crystalline room.
He sees clearly, and hopelessly desires,
A life that is not his.

Given the blindness of her self-possession,
The luminous vision revealed to his despair,
We look to both sides of the glass at once
And see no future in it.

These pure divisions hurt us in some realm
Of parable beyond belief, beyond
The temporal mind. Why is it sorrowful?
Why do we want them together?

Is it the spirit, ransacking through the earth
After its image, its being, its begetting?
The spirit sorrows, for what lovers bring
Into the world is death,

The most exclusive romance, after all,
The sort that lords and ladies listen to
With selfish tears, when she draws down the shade,
When he has turned away,

When the blind embryo with his bow of bees,
His candied arrows tipped with flower heads,
Turns from them too, for mercy or for grief
Refusing to be, refusing to die.

The Dial Tone

A moment of silence, first, then there it is.
But not as though it only now began
Because of my attention; rather, this,
That I begin at one point on its span
Brief kinship with its endless going on.

Between society and self it poses
Neutrality perceptible to sense,
Being a no man's land the lawyer uses
Much as the lover does: charged innocence,
It sits on its own electrified fence,

Is neither pleased nor hurt by race results
Or by the nasty thing John said to Jane;
Is merely interrupted by insults,
Devotions, lecheries; after the sane
And mad hang up at once, it will remain.

Suppose that in God a black bumblebee
Or colorless hummingbird buzzed all night,
Dividing the abyss up equally;
And carried its neither sweetness nor its light
Across impossible eternity.

Now take this hummingbird, this bee, away;
And like the Cheshire smile without its cat
The remnant hum continues on its way,
Unwinged, able at once to move and wait,
An endless freight train on an endless flat.

Something like that, some loneliest of powers
That never has confessed its secret name.
I do not doubt that if you gave it hours
And then lost patience, it would be the same
After you left that it was before you came.

Goldfish

The bearded goldfish move about the bowl
Waving disheveled rags of elegant fin
Languidly in the light; their mandarin
Manner of life, weary and cynical,

Rebukes the round world that has kept them in
Glass bubbles with a mythological
Decor of Rhineland castles on a shoal
Of pebbles pink and green. Like light in gin,

Viscous as ice first forming on a stream,
Their refined feathers fan them on to no
Remarkable purpose; they close their eyes
As, mouths reopening in new surprise
About their long imprisonment in O,
They cruise the ocean of an alien dream.

Polonius Passing through a Stage

Try to be yourself, they told the child.
I tried. Accumulating all those years
The blue annuities of silence some called
Wisdom, I heard sunstorms and exploding stars,
The legions screaming in the German wood—
Old violence petrifying where it stood.

The company in my Globe Theater rants
Its Famous Histories, the heroes fall
In ketchup and couplets. Ten heavenly don'ts
Botch up a selfhood, but where there's a Will
He's away. Rotting at ease, a ghostly doll—
What is that scratching on my heart's wall?

I tried to be myself. The silence grew
Till I could hear the tiniest Mongol horde
Scuffle the Gobi, a pony's felted shoe. . . .
Then from the fiery pit that self-born bird
Arose. A rat! The unseen good old man—
That sort of thing always brings the house down.

The View from Pisgah

Our God was to be a breath, and not a postcard
Of the sun setting over Niagara Falls:
"Wish you were here." Our God was first the breath
That raised a whirlwind in the desert dust,
The Wilderness of Sin. And then a word
Unspeakable, a stillness, and a standing stone
Set in the road; you would not raise a chisel
Upon that stone. Nothing but sky and sand
To purify a forbidden generation
Of Egypt's kitchens. In that wilderness
I've wandered for my forty years also,
Lifting mirages to break horizons, dreaming
Idolatries to alphabet the void,
Sending these postcards to the self at home:
Sunlight on pouring water; wish I were here.

Maiden with Orb and Planets

She stands now, shy among the destinies,
Daughter and mother of the silent crossings.
That is what beauty is, the petaled time
In a child's tomb, the basalt time that waits
In the Valley of the Kings, the swaying time
That smoothes the rivers through the summer nights
And polishes the stone and dulls the eye.
A china dynasty, the May fly's day,
Tremble to balance at her either hand,
And her blood moves as the dark rivers move,
While all the sailing stars pass and return.
Her stillness makes the moment of the world
Strike once, and that is what beauty is,
To stand as Agamemnon's daughter stood
Amid great armies waiting on the wind.

The First Point of Aries

After the morning of amazing rain
(How fiercely it fell, in slanting lines of light!)
A new breeze blew the clouds back to the hills,
And the huge day gloried in its gold and blue.

The road they walked was shoe-top deep in mud,
But the air was mild. And water of the spring,
The new, cold water, spread across the fields,
The running, the wind-rippled, the still-reflecting.

Life with remorseless joy possessed them then,
Compelling happiness beyond the power
Of prudence to refuse; perforce they gave
To splendor their impersonal consent.

What god could save them from this holy time?
The water, blinking in the sun's blue eye,
Watches them loiter on the road to death,
But stricken helpless at the heart with love.

The Dragonfly

Under the pond, among rocks
Or in the bramble of the water wood,
He is at home, and feeds the small
Remorseless craving of his dream,

His cruel delight; until in May
The dream transforms him with itself
And from his depths he rises out,
An exile from the brutal night.

He rises out, the aged one
Imprisoned in the dying child,
And spreads his wings to the new sun:
Climbing, he withers into light.

The Junction, on a Warm Afternoon

Out of the small domestic jungle,
The roadside scribble of wire and stick
Left over from last fall as we come
Into spring again, a slow freight
Incongruously rises into view.
The tall boxcars, rounding the bend,
Rattle their chains, and from the high
Cab of the engine, from the caboose,
The old men in caps and spectacles,
Gentle old men, some smoking pipes,
Nod with a distant courtesy,
Kindly and yet remote, their minds
On other things.

     Sunlight is warm
And grateful. The old railroad men
Are growing obsolete with the great
Engines whose demands they meet,
And yet they do not fail in their
Courtly consideration of the stranger
Standing in sunlight while the freight
Passes slowly along the line
To disappear among small trees,
Leaving empty the long, shining rails
That curve, divide, vanish, and remain.

Blue Suburban

Out in the elegy country, summer evenings,
It used to be always six o'clock, or seven,
Where the fountain of the willow always wept
Over the lawn, where the shadows crept longer
But came no closer, where the talk was brilliant,
The laughter friendly, where they all were young
And taken by the darkness in surprise
That night should come and the small lights go on
In the lonely house down in the elegy country,
Where the bitter things were said and the drunken friends
Steadied themselves away in their courses
For industrious ruin or casual disaster
Under a handful of pale, permanent stars.

These Words Also

There is her mother's letter on the table
Where it was opened and read and put down
In a morning remaining what it never was,
Remaining what it will not be again.

These words also, earth, the sun brings forth
In the moment of his unbearable brilliancy:
"After a night of drink and too much talk,
After the casual companions had gone home,
She did this. . . ." How the silence must have grown
Austere, as the unanswerable phone
Rang in a room that wanted to be empty.

The garden holds its sunlight heavy and still
As if in a gold frame around the flowers
That nod and never change, the picture-book
Flowers of somebody's forbidden childhood,
Pale lemony lilies, pansies with brilliant scowls
Pretending to be children. Only they live,
And it is beautiful enough, to live,
Having to do with hunger and reflection,
A matter of thresholds, of thoughtless balancings.

The black and gold morning goes on, and
What is a girl's life? There on the path
Red ants are pulling a shiny beetle along
Through the toy kingdom where nobody thinks.

Vermeer

Taking what is, and seeing it as it is,
Pretending to no heroic stances or gestures,
Keeping it simple; being in love with light
And the marvelous things that light is able to do,
How beautiful! a modesty which is
Seductive extremely, the care for daily things.

At one for once with sunlight falling through
A leaded window, the holy mathematic
Plays out the cat's cradle of relation
Endlessly; even the inexorable
Domesticates itself and becomes charm.

If I could say to you, and make it stick,
A girl in a red hat, a woman in blue
Reading a letter, a lady weighing gold . . .
If I could say this to you so you saw,
And knew, and agreed that this was how it was
In a lost city across the sea of years,
I think we should be for one moment happy
In the great reckoning of those little rooms
Where the weight of life has been lifted and made light,
Or standing invisible on the shore opposed,
Watching the water in the foreground dream
Reflectively, taking a view of Delft
As it was, under a wide and darkening sky.

At a Country Hotel

(a young widow with two pretty children)

"I watched the seeds come down this afternoon
Over the lawn, the garden and the gravel drive.
Even on the pool, where the children sailed
The paper boats you made them—paper boats
Among the lilies, frightening the frogs—
Seeds fell and were sailing.

"I never get tired of watching how the seeds
Break from that high sea of silver and green
Branches to tumble and drift, to glide and spin
Down. It makes me think of falling asleep,
The way people say, I mean, 'falling' asleep,
As if it were really a falling.

"Summer is gone, and the fire is almost out. . . .
How tired they were with playing! Will they dream
About their boats? Autumn is here, the night
Is rainy, with a cold wind; and still the seeds
Are falling, falling in darkness. Or else it is
The rain, that taps at the window."

It is late. He does not speak, will never speak.
She goes to the children sleeping, and he dreams
A kindly harbor, delicate with waves,
Where the tethered dories, rocking, rise and fall,
Until the high sail heightens, coming home
To landfalls of the lily and the ash.

The End of Summer School

At dawn today the spider's web was cold
With dew heavy as silver to the sight,
Where, kicked and spun, with clear wings befouled,
Lay in the shrouds some victims of the night.

This morning, too, as if they had decided,
A few first leaves came loose and drifted down
Still slopes of air; in silence they paraded
Their ominous detachment to the lawn.

How strange and slow the many apples ripened
And suddenly were red beneath the bough.
A master of our school has said this happened
"Quiet as grass can ruminate a cow."

And now the seeds go on their voyages,
Drifting, gliding, spinning in quiet storms
Obedient to the air's lightest laws;
And where they fall, a few will find their forms.

And baby spiders, on their shining threads,
The middle air make glisten gold all day;
Sailing, as if the sun had blessed their roads,
Hundreds of miles, and sometimes out to sea.

This is the end of summer school, the change
Behind the green wall and the steady weather:
Something that turns upon a hidden hinge
Brings down the dead leaf and live seed together,

And of the strength that slowly warps the stars
To strange harbors, the learned pupil knows
How adamant the anvil, fierce the hearth
Where imperceptible summer turns the rose.

Burning the Leaves

This was the first day that the leaves
Came down in hordes, in hosts, a great wealth
Gambled away over the green lawn
Belonging to the house, old fry and spawn
Of the rich year converted into filth
In the beds by the walls, the gutters under the eaves.
We thought of all the generations gone
Like that, flyers, migrants, fugitives.

We come like croupiers with rakes,
To a bamboo clatter drag these winnings in,
Our windfall, firstfruits, tithes and early dead
Fallen on our holdings from overhead,
And taxable to trees against our sin.
Money to burn! We play for higher stakes
Than the mere leaves, and, burdened with treasure, tread
The orbit of the tree that heaven shakes.

The wrath of God we gather up today,
But not for long. In the beginning night
We light our hoarded leaves, the flames arise,
The smell of smoke takes memory by surprise,
And we become as children in our sight.
That is, I think, the object of this play,
Though our children dance about the sacrifice
Unthinking, their shadows lengthened and cast away.

Elegy for a Nature Poet

It was in October, a favorite season,
He went for his last walk. The covered bridge,
Most natural of all the works of reason,
Received him, let him go. Along the hedge

He rattled his stick; observed the blackening bushes
In his familiar field; thought he espied
Late meadow larks; considered picking rushes
For a dry arrangement; returned home, and died

Of a catarrh caught in the autumn rains
And let go on uncared for. He was too rapt
In contemplation to recall that brains
Like his should not be kept too long uncapped

In the wet and cold weather. While we mourned,
We thought of his imprudence, and how Nature,
Whom he'd done so much for, had finally turned
Against her creature.

His gift was daily his delight, he peeled
The landscape back to show it was a story;
Any old bird or burning bush revealed
At his hands just another allegory.

Nothing too great, nothing too trivial
For him; from mountain range or humble vermin
He could extract the hidden parable—
If need be, crack the stone to get the sermon.

And now, poor man, he's gone. Without his name
The field reverts to wilderness again,
The rocks are silent, woods don't seem the same;
Demoralized small birds will fly insane.

Rude Nature, whom he loved to idealize
And would have wed, pretends she never heard
His voice at all, as, taken by surprise
At last, he goes to her without a word.

The Fall Again

It is the Old Man through the sleeping town
Comes oil dark to a certain lip, and breaks
By the white rain's beard the word he speaks,
A drunken Babel that spills upon a stone
And leaps in shatterings of light against
Its pouring fall, and falls again to spill
Asleep its dreaming strength along the kill
On those great sinews' curves twisted and tensed.

Between the vineyard and the drunken dark,
O sorrow, there the rainbow shines no more.
There promises are broken in the roar
Of that Old Man, the staggered Patriarch
And white beard falling naked to the floor
Ashamed, who was himself both Flood and Ark.

III *Vaudeville & Critique*

Lot Later

Vaudeville for George Finckel

I

It seems now far off and foolish, a memory
Torn at the hem from the fabric of a dream
In drunken sleep, but why was I the one?
God knows, there were no fifty righteous, nor
Ten righteous, in town just at that very moment;
Gone south for the winter, maybe. And moreover,
I wouldn't have been one of the ten or fifty
Or whatever, if there had been. Abraham
Stood up to Him, but not for me—more likely
For the principle of the thing. I've always been
Honest enough for this world, and respected
In this town—but to be taken by the hair
Like that, and lifted into that insane story,
Then to be dropped when it was done with me . . .
I tell you, I felt *used*.
                           In the first place,
I never knew the two of them were angels:
No wings, no radiance. I thought they might be students
Going from town to town, seeing the country.
I said "Come in the house, we'll have a drink,
Some supper, why not stay the night?" They did.
The only oddity was they didn't bother
With evening prayers, and that made me suspect
They might be Somebody. But in my home town
It doesn't take much; before I thought it out
People were coming round beating the door:
"Who you got in the house, let's have a party."
It was a pretty nice town in those days,

With always something going on, a dance
Or a big drunk with free women, or boys
For those who wanted boys, in the good weather
We used to play strip poker in the yard.
But just then, when I looked at those young gents,
I had a notion it was not the time,
And shouted through the door, "Go home, we're tired."
Nobody went. But all these drunks began
To pound the door and throw rocks at the windows
And make suggestions as to what they might do
When they got hold of the two pretty young men.
Matters were getting fairly desperate
By this time, and I said to those outside,
"Look, I got here my two daughters, virgins
Who never been there yet. I send them out,
Only my guests should have a peaceful night."
That's how serious the situation was.
Of course it wasn't the truth about the kids,
Who were both married, and, as a matter of fact,
Not much better than whores, and both the husbands
Knocking their horns against the chandeliers
Of my own house—but still, it's what I said.
It got a big laugh out there, and remarks,
Till the two young men gave me a nice smile
And stretched out one hand each, and suddenly
It got pitch dark outside, people began
Bumping into each other and swearing; then
They cleared away and everything was quiet.
So one young man opens his mouth, he says,
"You've got till sunrise, take the wife and kids
And the kids' husbands, and go. Go up to the hills."
The other says, "The Lord hath sent us to

Destroy this place" and so forth and so forth.
You can imagine how I felt. I said,
"Now look, now after all . . ." and my wife said,
"Give me a few days till I pack our things,"
And one of them looked at his watch and said,
"It's orders, lady, sorry, you've got till dawn."
I said, "Respectfully, gentlemen, but who
Lives in the hills? I've got to go, so why
Shouldn't I go to Zoar, which is a nice
Town with a country club which doesn't exclude
Jews?" "So go to Zoar if you want," they said.
"Whatever you do, you shouldn't look back here."
We argued all night long. First this, then that.
My son-in-laws got into the act: "You're kidding,
Things of this nature simply do not happen
To people like us." I said, "These here are angels,
But suit yourselves." The pair of them said, "We'll stay,
Only deed us the house and furniture."
"I wouldn't deed you a dead fish," I said,
"Besides, I'm going to take the girls along."
"So take," they said, "they weren't such a bargain."
The two visitors all this time said nothing,
They might as well not have been there. But I
Believed what I was told, and this, I think,
Makes all the difference—between life and death,
I mean—to feel sincerely that there's truth
In something, even if it's God knows what.
My poor old woman felt it too, that night,
She only couldn't hold it to the end.
The girls just packed their biggest pocketbooks
With candy and perfume; they'd be at home
Most anywhere, even in a hill.

At last

I knelt down and I spoke to my God as follows:
"Dear Sir," I said, "I do not understand
Why you are doing this to my community,
And I do not understand why, doing it,
You let me out. There's only this one thing,
So help me, that with all my faults I do
Believe you are able to do whatever you say
You plan to do. Myself, I don't belong
In any operation on this scale.
I've always been known here as a nice fellow,
Which is low enough to be or want to be:
Respectfully I ask to be let go
To live out my declining years at peace
In Zoar with my wife and the two kids
Such as they are. A small house will do.
Only I shouldn't be part of history."
Of course no one answered. One of them said:
"If you're about through, please get on your feet,
It's time to go." My daughters' gorgeous husbands
Were drinking on the porch before we left.

II

My relative Abraham saw it happen: the whole
Outfit went up in smoke, he said. One minute
There was the town, with banks and bars and grills
And the new sewage disposal plant, all looking
(he said) terribly innocent in the first light;
Then it ignited. It went. All those old pals
Gone up, or maybe down. I am his nephew,
Maybe you know, he had troubles himself,

With the maid, and his own son. That's neither here
Nor there. We'd been forbidden to look, of course,
But equally of course my old girl had to look.
She turned around, and in one minute there
She was, a road sign or a mileage marker.
By this time, though, I knew that what we were in
Was very big, and I told the kids Come on.
We didn't stop to cry, even. Also
We never went to Zoar. I began to think
How real estate was high, how I'd been told
To go up in the hills, and how I'd always
Wanted to live in the country, a gentleman
Like Abraham, maybe, and have my flocks
Or whatever you call them—herds. Well, I found out.
A cave, we lived in, a real cave, out of rock.
I envied those bums my son-in-laws, until
I remembered they were dead. And the two girls,
My nutsy kids, getting the odd idea
That the whole human race had been destroyed
Except for us, conceived—this word I love,
Conceived—the notion that they should be known
In carnal union by their poppa. Me.
Poor dear old Dad. Most any man might dream
About his daughters; darling and stupid chicks
As these ones were, I'd dreamed, even in daytime,
Such brilliant dreams. But they? They bought some booze,
Having remembered to bring money along,
Something I never thought of, considering
I was in the hand of God, and got me boiled.
And then—I'm told—on two successive nights
Arrived on my plain stone couch and—what shall I say?
Had me? I was completely gone at the time,

And have no recollection. But there they were,
The pair of them, at the next moon, knocked up,
And properly, and by their Dad. The kids
Turned out to be boys, Moab and Ben-Ammi
By name. I have been given to understand
On competent authority that they will father
A couple of peoples known as Moabites
And Ammonites, distinguished chiefly by
Heathenish ways and ignorance of the Law.
And I did this? Or this was done to me,
A foolish man who lived in the grand dream
One instant, at the fuse of miracle and
The flare of light, a man no better than most,
Who loves the Lord and does not know His ways,
Neither permitted the pleasure of his sins
Nor punished for them, and whose aging daughters
Bring him his supper nights, and clean the cave.

The Private Eye

To see clearly, not to be deceived
By the pretended burial of the dead,
 The tears of the bereaved,
 The stopped clock
 Or impenetrable lock,
Or anything that possibly was said
Simply to see who might have been misled;

To dig down deep enough to find the truth,
To penetrate and check, balance and sift,
 Pretending to be uncouth
 And a little dumb
 Till the truth come,
Till the proud and wicked give away their drift
Out of security—that is my gift,

To seem omnivorous in my belief,
Ready to swallow anything at first,
 (Knowing the corrupt chief
 Had rigged the raid
 So no arrest was made)
And, acting guileless as an infant nursed,
Believe in nothing till I get the worst.

I know what cannot possibly be known,
And never know I know it till the end.
 When justice must be done
 I give the word
 To the honestly bored
Survivors of my lust to apprehend,
And then, with the bourbon and the blonde, unbend.

To David, about His Education

The world is full of mostly invisible things,
And there is no way but putting the mind's eye,
Or its nose, in a book, to find them out,
Things like the square root of Everest
Or how many times Byron goes into Texas,
Or whether the law of the excluded middle
Applies west of the Rockies. For these
And the like reasons, you have to go to school
And study books and listen to what you are told,
And sometimes try to remember. Though I don't know
What you will do with the mean annual rainfall
On Plato's Republic, or the calorie content
Of the Diet of Worms, such things are said to be
Good for you, and you will have to learn them
In order to become one of the grown-ups
Who sees invisible things neither steadily nor whole,
But keeps gravely the grand confusion of the world
Under his hat, which is where it belongs,
And teaches small children to do this in their turn.

An Interview

Young man, the world's outside that door.
A theater full of risky charms,
With real and paranoid alarms:
Great heights for throwing oneself down
And shallows of a depth to drown—
Sawdust enough to save a clown.
Let others stay and mind the store:
What are you saving yourself for?

Young man, don't wait till you know more.
Too much the combat course around,
You'll never find the battleground.
The graves of some that played it cool,
And took no chance, nor looked the fool,
Are hid beneath the graduate school.
This music is to face before
You find out even what's the score.

So to the youth spoke old wisdom,
With leathery face and polished knob,
With golden smile and gold watch fob,
Arthritic knuckles, creaking knees,
And yet in this world well at ease
On sixty years of dignities.
The young man wondered, going home,
What was he saving himself from?

Gnomes

A SACRIFICED AUTHOR

Father, he cried, after the critics' chewing,
Forgive them, for they know not what I'm doing.

LOVE

A sandwich and a beer might cure these ills
If only Boys and Girls were Bars and Grills.

MINIM

The red butterflies are so beautiful!
But they will not stand still to be looked at.

Realities

She told him, "You were in my dream last night."
She was a bold one, anyhow, and he
Had never cared much for that kind; but now
She'd started something, he wondered.

The dream itself didn't amount to much.
The two of them had been in swimming, she said.
So that weekend they went out to the beach
To see what the dream had to say about that.

You metaphysicians, consider their four kids.
You couldn't hope for a nicer lot of kids
Or for a prettier split-level ranch-type home
To come from a dry swim in a dream.

Debate with the Rabbi

You've lost your religion, the Rabbi said.
    It wasn't much to keep, said I.
You should affirm the spirit, said he,
And the communal solidarity.
    I don't feel so solid, I said.

We are the people of the Book, the Rabbi said.
    Not of the phone book, said I.
Ours is a great tradition, said he,
And a wonderful history.
    But history's over, I said.

We Jews are creative people, the Rabbi said.
    Make something, then, said I.
In science and in art, said he,
Violinists and physicists have we.
    Fiddle and physic indeed, I said.

Stubborn and stiff-necked man! the Rabbi cried.
    The pain you give me, said I.
Instead of bowing down, said he,
You go on in your obstinacy.
    We Jews are that way, I replied.

To the Bleeding Hearts Association
of American Novelists

My grown-ups told me when I started out,
"You have to suffer in order to create."
It took me twenty years of stubborn doubt
Before I found the half-truth in all that.

We have so many fancy fellows now
That cannot leave their sufferings alone.
They spend their precious talents learning how
To paint a sigh, and decorate a groan.

Realistic till it hurts while it astounds
(And to conceal some small defects of art),
They slop their ketchup in the statue's wounds
And advertise that blood as from the heart.

I like those masters better who expound
More inwardly the nature of our loss,
And only offhand let us know they've found
No better composition than a cross.

The Poet at Forty

A light, a winged, & a holy thing,
Who if his God's not in him cannot sing.
Ah, Socrates, behold him here at last
Wingless and heavy, still enthusiast.

From the Desk of the Laureate:
For Immediate Release

Because Great Pan is dead, Astraea gone,
Because the singing has ceased upon Sion,
The Well at Helicon choked up with mud,
The Master of Songs tenders his resignation.

He cannot even do the Birthday Ode
For the Queen Mother, much less manage the
Elaborated forms of Elegy
And Epithalamion, when these fall due.

The Court will simply have to get along
As best it can on Chronicles in prose.
The Master regrets, but from this day the news
Must go uncelebrated in his song.

Although the pay was low, the hours long,
He wrote his wretched little works with love;
And if he will not have his lute restrung,
His reasons are the ones set forth above.

He has retired to the ancient horrible hotel
Where he can still afford to be a swell,
His nightly pony, a scotch whisky neat,
Brought by the servingman on squeaking feet.

Make Big Money at Home! Write Poems in Spare Time!

Oliver wanted to write about reality.
He sat before a wooden table,
He poised his wooden pencil
Above his pad of wooden paper,
And attempted to think about agony
And history, and the meaning of history,
And all stuff like that there.

Suddenly this wooden thought got in his head:
A Tree. That's all, no more than that,
Just one tree, not even a note
As to whether it was deciduous
Or evergreen, or even where it stood.
Still, because it came unbidden,
It was inspiration, and had to be dealt with.

Oliver hoped that this particular tree
Would turn out to be fashionable,
The axle of the universe, maybe,
Or some other mythologically
Respectable tree-contraption
With dryads, or having to do
With the knowledge of Good and Evil, and the Fall.

"A Tree," he wrote down with his wooden pencil
Upon his pad of wooden paper
Supported by the wooden table.
And while he sat there waiting
For what would come next to come next,
The whole wooden house began to become
Silent, particularly silent, sinisterly so.

On the Threshold of His Greatness, the Poet Comes Down with a Sore Throat

Enthusiasm is not the state of a writer's soul.—VALÉRY.[1]

For years I explored the pharmacopoeia
After a new vision. I lay upon nails
While memorizing the Seven Least Nostalgias.[2]
And I lived naked in a filthy cave,
Sneering at skiers, all one awful winter;
Then condescended, and appeared in tails
At the Waldorf-Astoria,[3] where I excelled
In the dancing of the Dialecticians' Waltz
Before admiring matrons and their patrons.

Those days, I burned with a hard, gemlike phlegm,
And went up like Excelsior[4] in a huff
Of seven-veiled symbols and colored vowels.
Flying from the alone to the Alone,[5]
My name appeared on every manifest
O.
Everything, Bhikkhus, was on fire.[6]
Things are so different now. My reformation,
Glittering o'er my fault.[7] . . . Anyhow,

---

[1] "Variety," tr. by Malcolm Cowley, in "An Introduction to the Method of Leonardo da Vinci."

[2] Ancient druidical chants of immense length. Also referred to, in some early writers, as "The Small End of the Egg of Wisdom."

[3] An hotel in New York City.

[4] A poem by Henry Wadsworth Longfellow.

[5] Plotinus, in Stephen Mackenna's translation.

[6] In the present tense in Buddha's Fire Sermon addressed to a thousand monks at Gaya Head in Magadha. See Henry Clarke Warren, "Buddhism in Translations" (Harvard, 1922), Ch. IV, Sec. 73. See also William Empson, "Poems" (London, 1935), and T. S. Eliot, "The Waste Land" (1922), Part III, "The Fire Sermon," ad fin. Bhikkhus = monks, or priests.

[7] Shakespeare, "Henry IV Part One," 1.2.236.

It's very quiet here at Monsalvat.[8]
The kids are singing in the cupola,[9]
But quietly. The good old psychopomp
Who comes to give my shots is terribly kind:
Procurasin at night in massive doses,
Repentisol next morning when I wake.
An unpretentious life, with late quartets
Among the early frescoes, a few friars
Asleep in their coffins[10] off to one side,
Angels adoring[11] where the jet planes wailed.
Evenings, we all eat from the same Grail.

Gin a body meet a body[12]
Under the boo[13]
   Under the bo
      Under the bodhi tree
—All is illusion,[14] all is vanity[14a]—
   Nobodhi there but me and me[15]

[8] The Grail Castle. Richard Wagner, "Parsifal," "Lohengrin." See also Nemerov, "The Melodramatists" (1949), pp. 155 & ff.

[9] T. S. Eliot, "The Waste Land," line 202: "Et O ces voix d'enfants, chantant dans la coupole!" Mr. Eliot's note attributes the line to Verlaine, "Parsifal," but probably the sentiment, in one form or another, goes back to antiquity. Cf. Kafka, "The Castle," where K., telephoning for permission to enter the Castle, hears in the receiver "the hum of countless children's voices—but yet not a hum, the echo rather of voices singing at an infinite distance."

[10] See James Joyce's celebrated story "The Dead," in "Dubliners."

[11] Painting by Fra Angelico in the National Gallery, London.

[12] Note the increased profundity of the Burns song in the new context.

[13] Cf. T. S. Eliot, "Fragment of an Agon": "Under the bam / Under the boo / Under the bamboo tree."

[14] The Buddha. [14a] Ecclesiastes. The collocation of these two representatives of Eastern and Western tradition, here at the collapse of the poem, may not be an accident.

[15] The Buddha achieved illumination and Buddhahood under the bo tree from the perception that all the forces of evil threatening him arose from within himself.

Metaphysics at mealtime gets in my hair.[16]

16 Wallace Stevens, "Les Plus Belles Pages": "Theology after breakfast sticks to the eye."

Notes by Cyril Limpkin, M.A. (Oxon.), Fellow in American literature at the University of Land's End, England.

NOTE ON NOTES: These notes have not the intention of offering a complete elucidation of the poem. Naturally, interpretations will differ from one reader to another, and even, perhaps, from one minute to the next. But because Modern Poetry is generally agreed to be a matter of the Intellect, and not the Feelings; because it is meant to be studied, and not merely read; and because it is valued, in the classroom, to the precise degree of its difficulty, poet and critic have agreed that these Notes will not merely adorn the Poem, but possibly supersede it altogether.

Metamorphoses

according to Steinberg

These people, with their illegible diplomas,
Their passports to a landscape full of languages,
Carry their images on banners, or become
Porters of pedestals bearing their own
Statues, or hold up, with and against gravity,
The unbalanced scrollwork of their signatures.
Thumbprints somehow get to be sanderlings,
And the cats keep on appearing, with an air
Of looking at kings even as they claw
Their way up the latticed cage of a graph,
Balance with fish, confront photographers
In family groups, or prowl music paper
Behind the staves.
             These in themselves, Master,
Are a great teaching. But more than for these
I am grateful for the lesson of the line,
That wandering divider of the world,
So casually able to do anything:
The extended clothesline that will carry trains,
For instance, or the lines of letters whose
Interstices vary the planes between
The far horizon and a very near nose.

The enchanted line, defying gravity and death,
Brings into being and destroys its world
Of marvelous exceptions that prove rules,
Where a hand is taken drawing its own hand,
A man with a pen laboriously sketches

Himself into existence; world of the lost
Characters amazed in their own images:
The woman elided with her rocking chair,
The person trapped behind his signature,
The man who has just crossed himself out.

Lion & Honeycomb

He didn't want to do it with skill,
He'd had enough of skill. If he never saw
Another villanelle, it would be too soon;
And the same went for sonnets. If it had been
Hard work learning to rime, it would be much
Harder learning not to. The time came
He had to ask himself, what did he want?
What did he want when he began
That idiot fiddling with the sounds of things.

He asked himself, poor moron, because he had
Nobody else to ask. The others went right on
Talking about form, talking about myth
And the (so help us) need for a modern idiom;
The verseballs among them kept counting syllables.

So there he was, this forty-year-old teen-ager
Dreaming preposterous mergers and divisions
Of vowels like water, consonants like rock
(While everybody kept discussing values
And the need for values), for words that would
Enter the silence and be there as a light.
So much coffee and so many cigarettes
Gone down the drain, gone up in smoke,
Just for the sake of getting something right
Once in a while, something that could stand
On its own flat feet to keep out windy time
And the worm, something that might simply be,
Not as the monument in the smoky rain
Grimly endures, but that would be
Only a moment's inviolable presence,

The moment before disaster, before the storm,
In its peculiar silence, an integer
Fixed in the middle of the fall of things,
Perfected and casual as to a child's eye
Soap bubbles are, and skipping stones.

IV *Endor*

DRAMA IN ONE ACT

Endor

The action takes place during one night, at first before,
and then within, the dwelling of the Witch of
Endor. One imagines this to be as much cave as house, with
a further recess, behind and above the fireplace, where
the apparitions are seen.

Outside the house. Saul, alone.

SAUL

How long it takes to learn a simple thing,
That when a man says absolutely, This
Thou shalt not, either to himself or others,
That is the thing he means to do, and will do
One day, as if to spite himself.

        That has been true
Of my whole life.

      After the old man died,
Samuel, my father in the spirit, and was buried
In Ramah, and all Israel wept for him
Except myself, I knew and I refused to know
That the spirit was gone from my kingship,
And my ordination taken away, the mantle torn.
I knew, and I refused to know, and I forbade
Witchcraft and divination in the kingdom,
Decreeing death on any who would scry
The future, or go questioning among the dead
By means of their familiar spirits. This I did,
Not wanting to know, and hoping not to know,
What he would speak with that rusty tongue of his
That could make even my God bitter to me.
I thought to be secure of the rebuke
Of dream or prophecy, letting the future fall
Day upon day until I died, after a life
Which would not be a destiny.

But now
God moves in darkness over against me, I feel it,
And like a man walking a strange road at night,
Sensing a fence before him, or a ditch,
I put my hand before my face, and grope and stumble
Where no obstacle is, but march in confidence
Over the river's edge. So to my shame
And in despair I have come secretly,
Not as a king, directed by ministers
Who snicker behind their sleeves because the king
Needs what the king forbids.
                              This is the place,
And they are in there now, bargaining with the woman
To gain my peace, my terrible peace.

                    (*He kneels, and beats with his fist on the ground.*)

Samuel, Samuel, cruel father, if you are
Under the world, hear me, speak, forgive
Saul who will be your obedient son, your king
In Israel.

                                        (*He rises.*)

          No, no, nothing. But yet
I know he listens there, and his skull wears still
The strict and secret smile of power which
Never forgives. Saul, Saul, you are a madman,
And sometimes in your heart you think that all,
Philistines, Israelites, and God himself,
Are gone, fled back and hidden away, so that you stand
On the world alone, stabbing at shadows.
Know, must you? What would you know? That you will die?
All men will die. That you will die tomorrow?
No, that's not it. You want to be at peace,
And get the old man's blessing from the deep

Sea of the grave. And as you have resolved,
Madman or not and King or not, so shall you do.

(He knocks at the door.)

You in there! Have you the woman of Endor?

*(The Witch of Endor comes forth, flanked
rather menacingly by the Minister and the
Commander.)*

THE WITCH

I've done nothing. I am an innocent woman,
I have no money. What do you mean to do to me?

SAUL

No harm. It is your help we are asking.
That discipline of yours among the dead,
Who tell you secrets, and with empty eyes
Peer into things to come. That is my need.

THE WITCH

I do not understand what you or these men mean.
I think you have mistaken me for someone else,
Or you have heard a scandal spread about me
(As happens to a woman all alone),
To make you think I have the second sight
Or power with the dead.

COMMANDER

                Now that's enough.
We know about you, and there's no mistake.

MINISTER *(aside, to Saul)*

The woman is shy, my Lord, thinks we are the law,
And will admit to nothing. You shall do best,
I think, by kindness, not command; and remember,
If she should recognize you for the king,
We shall get nothing from her.

SAUL

Madam,

It's not for you to be afraid of us.
The powers you possess, which are well known,
Command more than respect. I am quick to say
I fear them. But I also need them, and
I am ready to pay you well for what you do.

THE WITCH

Supposing you are, that's still not good enough,
For if I had those "powers," as you call them,
I'd be a fool to show them off to strangers
Who may for all I know be spies. King Saul
Forbids this business to be practiced, and many
Who traded in the future and with spirits
Have died of his forbidding. Would you trap me?
But even so, I'm not the woman you believe me,
And have no talents that way. I am a widow,
I live quietly, there is no mystery about me.

SAUL

We have come here by night. My need is great.
What must I do to make you trust me?

COMMANDER

Since kindness will not do it,
Look, woman, at this sword, look hard at it.
Here is the immediate threat. Do you wish to die?

MINISTER

Now what will that accomplish? This is not
The situation for your soldierly bluster.

THE WITCH

It is a foolish threat. Suppose I were
The woman that you think me, would my death

Be any use to you? It's not that way
I fear you, any of you, for it comes to me
When I look hard at you three strong men
That I shall outlive some of you at least.

SAUL

What do you mean? You speak
As though of something certain. Tell me, then.
You cannot mean to say what you have said
And leave it at hints and guesses? What you tell
I will bear quietly, I swear it. And I swear
No hurt shall come to you, neither by law
Nor from the bitterness of all our hearts
If what you tell is doom.

     (He kneels to her; the two courtiers turn away, half-
        smiling, in respect and scorn and shame.)

THE WITCH

What word of power will you swear it by?

SAUL *(kneeling)*

By the Lord God of Israel, I swear there shall
No punishment happen to thee for this thing.

THE WITCH

A mighty word to take upon the tongue.
You are a strange man, possibly a foolish one.
I like your foolishness, and only for that
I will believe your word. Come in with me,
These others may remain behind.

      (Saul and the Witch enter the house.)

MINISTER

I am the king's first minister.
The position of personal servant to the great
Is a delicate one, requiring of a man

A keen sense not merely of where the bread is buttered,
The pot sweetened, or the fat in the fire,
But of the balance to be kept
Between his person and his office.
To serve the lusts of majesty, or its rage,
Or childish fear; to superintend
The concubine or the assassin
With equal secrecy and poise,
Is not a weakling's job. You need
To be a hypocrite, a sycophant, a pimp,
And, at the same time, absolutely loyal,
Utterly sincere. To be a king's servant
Is to have immense power, and know enough to know
That one will never use it where it matters.

COMMANDER

I am the commander of the king's guard,
And my profession is fidelity
Ending in death. My only power
Is the power of blind obedience.
I and my forces do not matter until disaster,
And then we do not matter. That is the meaning
Of spit and polish and golden breastplate,
The pomp and honor of parade, the armed
Solemnity at the king's riding out or at
His keeping court—that we shall be there at the end,
To demonstrate how men must meet the end.

MINISTER

So when King Saul drew me aside and said
"Find me a witch, a wizard, anyone
Who hears God, reads the future, traffics with the dead,"
I did as I was told. I did not remind him of his law

Forbidding people of that sort to practice
Their mortal arts in Israel, I simply said
"My Lord, there is such a one, a woman,
Living at Endor." Neither did he ask
Me how I knew. It is assumed between us
That I know what I must.

COMMANDER

I have been with King Saul for many years,
Since the establishing of the Kingdom,
Have been a faithful servant, have kept
(As we say in the forces) my mouth closed
And my bowels open—which is to say, I have endured
His sulks and rages, periods of baseless suspicion
And insane favoritism, and even—what was harder—
The concerts of effeminate music on the harp
To which in certain moods he is so partial.
Yet I have seen in him a good commander and my king.

MINISTER

You have been honored for it. So have I.
And in the fat times, it went easy. One might overlook
His temper, uncertainly swaying back and forth
Between an arrogance which made all things
Look possible, and melancholy so deep
He would not eat. One paid that price,
But in return one had a place, and not the lowest,
In something alive and likely to go on.
Tonight it is different.

COMMANDER

Tonight we may be near the end.
The armies of the Philistine, increased
With allies, and among them the young man David

79

(Who serves the King of Gath, for his own ends),
Lie in the camp at Shunem, while our force
Has occupied Gilboa. All the space between
Lies in the balance of tomorrow's battle.
I do not fear a fight, or the chance of death,
But this new desperation of the king's
Makes me uneasy. Why are we here
On this lonely hillside, consulting with a woman,
Ourselves and the king disguised?

MINISTER

It is as though the end already exists
Out there, blindly, in darkness, while we,
Like blind men, stumble toward it.
Trust me, I know the king, I know
His power has gone out of him, poor man.
Samuel destroyed him over Amalek,
When Saul refused to slaughter the survivors.
And since that time, before the old man died,
He secretly anointed the boy David,
Gave him the kingship under God, so that
Saul holds this realm only by personal force,
The blessing on him gone.

COMMANDER

                              I too have felt,
Having a professional sense for such things,
That I am on the wrong side. Nevertheless,
Morale must be kept up, and the king is wrong
To let even his trusted servants see
The fall of things hanging upon a woman's word.

MINISTER

I wonder what she can be telling him?
The future . . . does it already exist,

Waiting for us to come marching along
And fill its outlines with our flesh and blood?

COMMANDER

The soldier is not paid to think that way.

MINISTER

I know, the soldier is not paid to think.
And maybe no one knows how God
Creates tomorrow. What could He create it from?
Unless it's there already? Now, supposing
Tomorrow to be there, and knowledge possible,
Should a man want it? Have you asked yourself
Whether you would rather, all things considered,
Foreknow the future or go at it blind?

COMMANDER

Brother, that is a question
Only civilians ask. Blind, blind is better.
Where would obedience be, and discipline,
When once the end was guaranteed? If a good end,
No one would bother fighting, and that would turn it bad.
If bad to begin with, no one would bother fighting,
Since he might better die drunk and in bed on the same day.
No, let me be blind, if I'm to have a choice.

MINISTER

The question is, though, whether you and I
Will have a choice? Sometimes
A close association with the mighty
Requires that one suffer the inordinate pressures
That march with power; and then, although a man
Is but a man, with a life and a death, no more,
One must endure as though one had a destiny

In the direct glare of God's eye. How shall I,
Civilian as you say, face up to that?

COMMANDER

We in the service are not commanded to believe
That anyone foretells the future. It is
A superstition, and, besides, would be
Intolerable if it were not.

(*A cry of rage from Saul within.*)

The king calls out!

There is some danger!

MINISTER

From the woman? More likely
She has crossed him somehow, and got his temper up.
Still, let us look helpful.

COMMANDER

Come, quickly!

(*As the two courtiers enter, the curtains of the
forestage part disclosing the interior of the
Witch's dwelling: a small, shadowy room waveringly
illuminated by a fire at the back, yet giving a
dark impression of great depth; another room off
to one side.*)

SAUL (*to the Witch*)

God's thunder smite you for a liar and fraud,
And let me be the instrument! Have I none about me
But flatterers, deceivers by sweet words?

COMMANDER

My Lord!

MINISTER

Patience, Saul.

THE WITCH

Protect me, he is the king! I knew at once.
Remind him, gentlemen, that he swore an oath
No harm would come to me.

SAUL

Must I be taken in by fortune tellers' tricks?

MINISTER

My Lord, what has the woman done?

SAUL

She has mistaken me what I am.
For when I said to her the name of Samuel
She cries at once: The King! It is the King!

(*He imitates the woman's voice.*)

O sir, she says, no need to bring him up,
I see in the stars, I scry in the dark water,
I dreamed last night, I read in the cracked shell
Of a tortoise and from the guts of a frog. . . .
And whatnot else she babbled on, from fear,
All tending to establish endless life
And all good fortune to her kind King Saul,
Her merciful King Saul, whose mercy would
Surely protect her from a witch's death.
I say, she has misjudged me what I am!

MINISTER (*aside*)

We know that tone too well. And a king's rage
Must run its course. The end of it, for him,
Is black despair, he punishes himself.

SAUL

Ha ha! She feared to die for being a witch,
And the joke of it is that she shall die
For failing to be witch enough.

THE WITCH

Your oath!

You swore upon the name of the living God.

MINISTER and COMMANDER

My Lord. My Lord.

SAUL

Beware. My business now is with the woman.
My dear, now that you know I am the king,
You must do what I ask, your mystery,
For nothing less will do. Deal honestly,
My oath protects you. Once more put me off
With prophecies of long life and success,
As flatterers do, as you have tried to do,
Your life pays for it.

It is the truth I want.

THE WITCH

And must the truth be always bitter, Saul?

SAUL

Already I suspect, and come to you
For visible certainties. It is not death
We fear, but going to
Forsaken actions, while God laughs in hiding.
Ends can be faced, but not the emptiness
Of ignorance, where folly tries conclusions
With what is already done. I say again,
Bring me up out of the grave the old wizard,
Samuel, I mean, the last judge in Israel.
Say that his king would question him. Say that.

COMMANDER

My Lord?

SAUL

Yes?

COMMANDER

If my Lord please, I have been a faithful servant,
And never one to put himself forward, either.
But now there is something I should like to say.

MINISTER

The military mind, faced with the dead,
Is getting embarrassed.

COMMANDER

That's not what I mean.

SAUL

You may speak.

COMMANDER

Consider a moment, my Lord, if it is good
To know what happens next. For once the dead
Shall rise and speak, are not our wills enthralled
Under the lips of dust? Better to doubt.
What can the dead say other than despair,
Since they know nothing else? No, better doubt,
And let tomorrow, like any other day,
Come as it will and go as it will. What are
The few more hours till our battle is drawn?
We should be resting, and readying ourselves,
Not seeking the speculations of a ghost.
Above all else, let us not start to fight
In the conviction of defeat.

SAUL

I see
You too believe we are to be defeated.

MINISTER

    I'm sure my colleague does not entertain
    That treasonable thought. He merely means,
    My Lord, and he has reason on his side,
    That the will to fight is delicate as a girl,
    Who, once her first resistance weakens, comes near
    Corrupting altogether. If the end
    Inevitably must be thus and such, it might
    Be well to live an hour or two more
    Without the knowledge. Someone like myself,
    Civilian to the core, may hear the truth
    Or not, it hardly matters; but the soldier,
    While this is going on, might best
    Stand in the corner and stuff his fingers in his ears.

SAUL

    You are eloquent. But I have lived that way
    Too long. When Samuel turned away from me,
    That bitter, unforgiving man of God,
    I in my rage drove David from my side,
    And wanted to destroy him. After that,
    When Samuel died, the voice of God fell silent
    Within me and around me, and my realm,
    Wanting in metaphysical love and truth,
    Shriveled inside, a kingdom dry as sand
    Whose king was but a stone in the spirit's path
    From the true father to the anointed son.
    Thenceforth, not wanting to hear the Word of God,
    I stoppered up the ways of access, dreams
    And prophecies, and banned the necromancers.
    And then, when I began to want again
    The painful consolation of the truth,
    My dreams were dumb, and divination failed.

So now I come, since the great gate is shut,
Round to the kitchen door, that the black art
And traffic in the filthy beds of death
May bring me to my difficult peace.

                                          Woman,
Begin your spells.

THE WITCH
  Patience, my Lord. For all my preparations,
  It's hard. They don't always want to come up,
  And those that do come may not want to speak.
  They're sullen, the old ones in the earth, sullen.
  But I have the mastery of them in the end.

> (*She crouches before the fire. Her procedures
> consist in mutterings and croonings not intel-
> ligible to us, and in throwing powders and
> liquids from various bottles on the fire.
> This should not look awesome, or even very
> impressive; after all, it is only a sort
> of cookery.*)

MINISTER
  It lowers one's opinion of the dead
  To think they rise to a rigmarole like this.

SAUL
  Be quiet.

> (*He is watching intently over the woman's shoulder;
> the others are somewhat withdrawn.*)

COMMANDER (*whispering*)
  What can this bring us but regret?

MINISTER (*whispering*)
  It's rather interesting, though, isn't it?

COMMANDER

It is horrible, it is revolting.

MINISTER

Come now, surely the soldier cannot shirk
Inspecting his professional results?

>(*The Witch gives a long, low cry.*)

SAUL

What have you seen?

THE WITCH

I see gods ascending out of the earth.
They go, they go, like bats behind the flame.
And now, look, it is an old man, his head
Is shrouded in a mantle.

>(*Samuel appears.*)

SAUL (*thrusting her aside*)

>>It is Samuel.

>(*He kneels at the fire.*)

Father and Judge, forgive. Have pity.

SAMUEL

Why have you disquieted me, to bring me up?

SAUL

The Philistines have come against me, and the Lord
Forsaken me, he answers me not by prophets
Nor comes to me in dreams. Father, I call to you
That you will tell me what thing I must do
To make whole the mantle of this land
You tore from me at Gilgal, when you killed
The King of Amalek. Father, I bow my head.
Yours is the power.

SAMUEL

The power is the Lord's.
I sleep in the dirt of the earth, you ask in vain,
Seeing that God has turned his face from you
And torn the kingdom from your hand, and given
The mantle of it to the shepherd David.
Out of your disobedience, Saul, it came,
Because you turned in the hand of power, because
You did not His vengeance and execution on Amalek,
Therefore the Lord has splintered you against a stone
And taken another instrument.

SAUL

What must I do?

SAMUEL

The time to do is gone; what you must suffer
Is what is already done. The Philistine
Already hangs your armor in the house
Of Ashtaroth, your body from the wall at Beth-shan.
Tomorrow you will be with me.

(*As the apparition fades on these words, Saul utters
a cry and falls fainting.*)

COMMANDER (*kneeling beside him*)

My Lord! Comfort, my Lord. Don't give way.
It was a trick of the fire that we saw,
The woman's voice we heard, seeming to come
From the angle of the wall, and our brains,
Troubled between fear and desire,
Perfected the illusion. Now, my Lord,
You can't believe in that, you can't believe
Tomorrow has already come and gone
In a kitchen fireplace.

SAUL

What does it matter
What I believe, what you believe? Tomorrow
Is like a town at the end of a long road
Across a desert country. First in mirages
Its towers and its walls appear, as if
In a dream, and tremble high above the ground
In a shaken air, but then, as we go on,
The real town too appears, and no less real
Although we think it another trick of the light.

COMMANDER

But he is gone, my Lord. Open your eyes.
The fire sputters there, nothing but fire.
It was illusion, or it was a dream.

MINISTER

And dreamed by all of us at once, and waking.

SAUL

I feel that I have slept. My legs are weak,
My head is heavy. Did you hear him speak?
You heard him speak. My body on the wall,
He said, down at Beth-shan. I should like to sleep
A little more. It is a weakness in me,
And I would sleep until it passes.

THE WITCH

If the king wishes to rest, there is a couch
In the further room.

COMMANDER

Come then, my Lord, get up.

Give me a hand (*to the Minister*),
Don't stand there dreaming. And you, my good woman,

Prepare what you have in the way of food and drink.
I'll stay with the king a while.

> (*The Commander and the Minister help
> the king into the other room.*)

THE WITCH (*singing*)
Between the living and the dead,
Between the living and the dead
   My traffic and my art.
   The womb in the head,
   The grave in the heart.
How time is born of time, the seed
Born of the tree, the tree of the seed.
They dream each other, the living and the dead,
In the grave of my heart, the womb of my head.

> (*The Minister returns.*)

THE MINISTER
My colleague is staying there to guard the king.
This is the kind of emergency he finds
Acceptable, for he can deal with it,
Bring blankets and get food. It's curious
How much even of warfare is housekeeping.
Of course he has to stay and guard the king,
That is his job. And yet I should have thought
That if the king is destined to die tomorrow
He would be perfectly safe tonight. My dear,
You are a clever woman, or maybe a deep one,
I don't know which. How do you do these things?

> (*During the following conversation the Witch
> is preparing food and drink.*)

THE WITCH
I do nothing. And yet there is nothing
Which is not done.

MINISTER

Mystical talk.
I've never understood that kind of thing,
Nor greatly cared to. And I'm not pressing you for
Professional secrets. But isn't it rather odd?
The king will die tomorrow. Now we know
The king will die tomorrow, which means, I guess,
Defeat, confusion, all the baggage lost,
Some towns burnt down, the flocks and herds let stray
All over the place . . . and at the very least
The end of an order of existence which
I shall be sorry to see go. It is
An inconvenience, to put it no more strongly.
You think me, perhaps, unfeeling, but that's not so.
What is it possible to feel? We've had
The experience, but not the weight of it.
For here I am, and here you are, it is
As though nothing whatever had happened. That
May be the most uncanny thing of all,
That nothing, really, has happened.
Tell me the future. I suppose
That David will be King of Israel?

THE WITCH

I do not know the future. Only, when I stare
Into the fire, I see strange images rising.
They mean nothing to me. My power is,
Such as it is, that others, who look with me
Into the flames, beyond the flames, can see
As I can see. But it's for them to say
If what they see is future or is past;
And what it means, if it means anything,
It means to them, never to me.

MINISTER

Then stare with me into the fire, for I
Must have a fate also.

THE WITCH

Must you?

MINISTER

I'm wondering if perhaps my fate will be
Desertion, and joining the Philistines
Before tomorrow's battle. That is the fate
I should like to see about. Without wishing
To give offense, however, I may point out
How tactless it would be to mention that
Before the king. Let us agree, dear lady,
That I was only thinking aloud.

THE WITCH

I think
Men of your sort, though they have lives and deaths,
Never have fates. Maybe because they have
Their cleverness instead, their light, dry minds
Which blow in the wind of fortune back and forth,
They can have many meanings, no one meaning.

MINISTER

I have heard that thought before. And it is true,
I've always been a great believer
In my own comfort first, and let the great storms,
That blow the great men down, find me in bed.
One has the temperament one's born with, though.
It happens that I'm not a king, it happens
That I never wanted to be a king, and so
We live as we may. And yet I have the courage
To stare into the fire, if you will.

THE WITCH
It is no matter to me.

> (*They crouch down before the fire, the Witch doing
> her work as before. Presently, behind the fire and
> above it, at a distance and in bright light, appear
> Saul and his Commander. They are armed and dressed
> in armor, and the king wears the crown.*)

SAUL
It is over, it is done, my power gone
As blood into the ground, where my blood soon
Must follow. Now the noise of battle is drawn
Northward, away, and now we stand alone
With nothing to command. The field is won
Against us. Let not the Philistine women
Who follow the armies, finding me alive,
Abuse and torture me before they kill me.
My mind is clear, I keep a high resolve,
With nothing left of kingship but its courage,
Which I shall not need long.
Therefore, your last service.

> (*Offers his sword.*)

Come, man,
I close my eyes, I wait, let it be done
What you are sworn to do, for this is the end
Of all, as Samuel foresaid.

COMMANDER (*takes the sword*)
Lord, I cannot.
My love, my loyalty, are to your life,
And not your death. This hand stiffens with fear
And will not move against the king its master.

SAUL

Come, the sword, the sword. How long must courage
Endure before it wins? I wait, the king
Waits on his servant. Kill me, quickly, and then
You may yourself, or else do what you like,
Live, if you like. Ah, faithless. Give me the sword.

COMMANDER

My Lord, I cannot.

SAUL (*takes the sword from him*)

Then I must do all
For myself alone. Whatever I have known,
Whatever I have been, the child, the man,
And all the sights my closing eyes have seen,
Meant but this moment only, and then
The weary, painful world shall be withdrawn
And be as a stone.

(*He falls on his sword.*)

It is over, it is done.
See, Samuel, my father, David more than my son,
I make an end of time.

COMMANDER

My Lord, I was unable.
I stood like a stone, no matter what I vowed,
I could not think the end, and could not act.
Forgive me, Lord.

SAUL

Kill . . . in the name of mercy, kill, the sword
Is like a fire in me, and I live,
The great pain I am skewered with
Will make me live. Be quick, kill.

COMMANDER (*drawing his own sword*)

Now my Lord forgive me, but I will. I must.

(*He stabs Saul.*)

It is done. But how suddenly he stares,
As though no man were there at all, no king.
He is at peace. But I? No, no, I cannot.
And if I missed, as he did, mortality
At the single stroke, who's here to do for me
What I have done for him, open the gate
And ease the passage? No, I cannot die.
Besides, with the king's death this disaster
Is finished. Those who remain, who wants their lives?
I shall live out my time peaceably, perhaps.
But to live, to live in shifting times like these,
A man must use whatever comes to hand.
Forgive this, master. Had we any hope,

(*He takes the crown.*)

Even of dying in battle, nobly, I
Would keep my place beside you. As things are,
I go to find King David, and to him
Tender my services, with your crown. I swear,
Dear Lord, I never thought it would be thus.
You dead men are well out of it, the living
Must do what their necessity demands.

(*The scene in the fireplace fades.*)

MINISTER

So. Military honor, in the end,
Is as careful of its precious skin as any
Dry clever mind in the world. Many thanks,
Dear lady, for the lesson, but don't you think,
If destiny depends on keeping faith,

He has as little right to one as I?
These clanking heroes lord it over us,
With their lantern jaws and tiny brains, year in,
Year out. We may not be so clever, they say,
But at least we shall know how to die. And then
They don't know how to die. Disgusting fools.

THE WITCH
Look once again into the fire. See!

MINISTER
I know him! It is the young man David, once
The favorite, whom Saul drove into exile.

> (*In the fire, as before. King David, with soldiers.*
> *Enter to him the Commander holding the crown.*)

DAVID
Who is this man? I know his face, it is
King Saul's Commander of the Guard.

COMMANDER (*kneels, holding forth the crown*)
My Lord, David, be King in Israel!

DAVID
You tell me thus that Saul is dead?

COMMANDER
                                    He is dead.

DAVID
You come to tell me this, and hope for favor?
How did he die?

COMMANDER
After the battle broke around us, and
Those who were able fled, King Saul and I
Stood on the Mount Gilboa among the dead.
He asked for his death at my hand, but I,

Sworn to it though I was, refused to strike,
For pity, for love, for fear. He took the sword
And fell against the point, but he could not
Rid himself of his life, nor had he strength
To strike himself again. He begged his death,
And because his pain was terrible to see,
Unwillingly I finished what he had begun.

DAVID

He was to me a father and a friend,
Though of an angry and unhappy nature.
Why were you not afraid to lift your hand
Against the Lord's Anointed? and to shed
That sacred blood?

COMMANDER

            It was for pity, Lord.
He would have died of the wound, after much pain.
I did it out of love.

DAVID

The crown. You bring me that too out of love?

COMMANDER

My Lord, I could not leave it to be found
By the Philistine. Now it belongs to you.
I did my duty as I saw it, and
I hope I may find favor in your eyes.

DAVID

Give me the crown.

                          (*He puts on the crown.*)

            Ah, my father and friend,
The beauty of Israel is slain
On her high places. How are the mighty fallen!

As for this man, soldier, stand over him   (*to a soldier*)
And strike him till he die.

COMMANDER

> Lord, have mercy!

DAVID

His blood be on his head. For his own mouth
Has testified against him: I have slain
The Lord's Anointed.

> (*Soldiers kill the Commander.*)

Ye mountains of Gilboa, let there be
Upon ye neither rain nor dew, for here
The shield of Saul is vilely cast away,
As though he had not been anointed with oil.
It comes to me that I shall make a psalm
To be a requiem, when the daughters of Israel
Shall weep for Saul. . . .
Daughters of Israel, weep over Saul
Who clothed you in scarlet, in ornaments of gold.
And who is slain in the high and lonely place.
How are the mighty fallen, and the weapons of war broken.

> (*The scene in the fire fades.*)

MINISTER

So that is how it ended. Strange, and sad,
And dreamy, as though it were already
An old story. After all, the man of war
Died of the war. And that, to me, is justice.
He got what he deserved, though, don't you think?
And David's indifference was admirable,
I thought, though cold. These poets!
Real people scarcely exist for them.

> (*The Witch shrugs, rises, not speaking, and begins
> to set a table in the other corner.*)

I wish there had been something there for me,
Something to tell me what I ought to do,
What I will do. What shall I be doing
Tomorrow at this time? How queer that is:
It would not be what I *will* do, but what
I had already done.
                    Those two in there,
They are already dead, then. Don't you think
It may be just a trifle embarrassing,
For us, I mean? How does one speak to people
Whose bodies one has seen dead in a field?

THE WITCH

I did, of all that was demanded, all
I could. The images came and went, came
And went as they would. The fire is almost out.
It will do you no good, you'll find, to speak
To them of what you saw.

MINISTER

                    You're quite certain
You can't see anything to do with me?

THE WITCH

It would be a kindness, sir, for you to fetch
A few more sticks from outside, for the fire.
It's almost out.

MINISTER

                    I see, you'll tell me nothing.
All right, then. We must keep these dead men warm.

                              (*He goes out.*)

THE WITCH (*knocks at the door of the further room*)
  If my Lord please, I have something to eat,
  And some wine to settle the stomach after his
  Experience.

      (*She listens for a moment, then withdraws from the door.*)

  It's no great trouble, if you have the gift,
  Seeing the future. It comes as it comes, that's all.
  But wanting to! I never understood
  What made them want to. I have never asked
  To see my future, and I never did.
  Living in time has warmth and decency,
  It's like a sheep-lined coat in a cold night.

      (*Saul and the Commander enter from the other room.*)

SAUL
  I have to die. I have to die tomorrow.
  The understanding of it, that's not it.
  But to have torn open the mercy of time
  And seen a corpse in a pit. . . .
  What is this flesh, that I should give it food
  Or let it sleep? There will be time to sleep.

THE WITCH
  My Lord, here are both meat and wine.
  Let nature's comfort work as it will,
  And as it must. The strength that carries us
  Never believed in death, does not believe
  In death, but wants what any child wants.

COMMANDER
  The woman is right, my Lord. And think that now,
  Knowing the worst that is given men to know,
  The hour and occasion of their end,

You have the certainty all seek, the thing
That courage and constancy train us to meet.

> (*Saul lets himself be led to the table, but sits
> staring into the fire. The Minister enters with
> an armful of wood, with which the woman builds
> the fire up.*)

MINISTER

So cold the night! It must be nearly dawn.
We should be starting back.

SAUL

My body from the wall, he said, the wall
At Beth-shan. Look at me, all of you.
I am brave, I face it, I look it in the eye
As a king should. My body hanging there,
In chains? Even on hooks. Let it happen.
The skin dries in the sun, blackens and splits,
The birds eat through the eyes, into this mind
That thinks these thoughts, and the rain, the rain
Washes the wounds, the wind blows, and the sun
Shines on this thing, this bag of blood and bones
You tell me I must feed (as I would a horse,
To carry me over a cliff), this brute of power
That once pretended to be a child, a man,
A king; that went in to women, that fathered sons,
That lusted helpless in the heat of life,
That maddened at times, and cried easily at music—

COMMANDER

This feeds the feelings, Lord, you ought to starve.

THE WITCH

Drink the wine, good sir. Past help, past tears.
See if you don't feel better after a cup of wine.

(Saul drinks unwillingly at first. During what follows,
however, he and the others, without making a particular
point of it, apply more and more to the food and drink,
which they consume while talking.)

SAUL

Now I remember how at Havilah,
After the battle, Agag the King of Amalek
Said to me, Surely the bitterness of death
Is past? Poor man, he looked me in the eye
Bravely enough, but I could smell the fear,
I heard the tremor in the voice.
I would have spared,
Because one can be sick to death of death
When the fighting is over, and besides, what use
Would one more corpse have been? But Samuel,
Taking the knife in his own hand, slaughtered
The King of Amalek before the Lord,
Our God, whose mercy and lovingkindness on Israel
Demanded blood. How long ago that is!
And did my disobedience on that day,
My disobedience treasured up in God
So many years, bring me to Endor now?
To death tomorrow? Have I lived, then,
Narrowly in the spaces of a dream,
Where motion only seemed to move? Because
We read the story as the scroll unfolds,
We think the end unwritten yet.

COMMANDER

My Lord,
What can men do with time? We all must die.
And what remains is now to face it nobly,

And in the soldier's manner. For remember,
No matter what we know, it is up to us
To set a good example to the men.

MINISTER

Aha!

COMMANDER

And what does that mean?

MINISTER

O, nothing, nothing whatever. I was thinking
Of something else.

SAUL

You tell me all men die.
A noble sentiment, I drink to it.
But neither of you has heard, as I have heard,
The moment of the sentence in advance.

COMMANDER

Respectfully, sir, but you slight my honor.
The sentence falls on me as well as you,
For I am sworn to follow where you lead,
Even to the end.

MINISTER

Now that simply is not so.

COMMANDER

You may be unaware how dangerous
That observation is. You will think twice
Before repeating it.

THE WITCH

I warned you, sir,
Against the speech you are about to speak.
There's malice in it, and some danger, too.

SAUL

What he knows, let him speak it now.

MINISTER

I must regret that I may not, like you,
Indulge myself in brilliant attitudes
About what is to come. Knowledge forbids it.
I make the statement of a simple fact.
The woman showed it to me in the flames,
And it is this:
The king will die tomorrow by your hand.

SAUL

Minister, you exceed your authority.
We do not think of you among the prophets.

MINISTER

Not only that, but you will fail to follow.
Beholding the king dead, a little thought,
A tiny thought, will come between you and
That loyalty which you regard so highly.
Briefly, you are to give the crown to David.

SAUL

Can this be true?

MINISTER

I saw it where you saw the ancient rise
To speak what you were better not to hear.

SAUL

Shall I believe this? Am I sitting here
At table, drinking wine and breaking bread
With a traitor and my executioner?

COMMANDER

My Lord, you know my character.

MINISTER

And I, you see, I know your destiny.
I'm sorry for you both. But there it is.

COMMANDER

You must know, Minister, that you have made
An intolerable accusation, one that stains
A long life's honor. It demands your blood.

(*He draws a knife.*)

MINISTER (*backing away*)

Please understand, it is no accusation.
I have only great respect for your courage,
And was surprised, I may say even shocked,
To see what it will come to in the end.

COMMANDER

My Lord, permit me to kill this person first—

MINISTER

Stop, stop, you haven't heard how the story ends.

COMMANDER

Permit me to kill this person first, I say,
And then, because I cannot live dishonored
And under the suspicion of my king,
I beg to be put to death, sir, at once, by you.

MINISTER

It's no use, don't you see. He cannot do it.

SAUL

Be careful of saying cannot to a king.

MINISTER

Great king, not I forbid, but destiny.
If you are fated to receive your death
At this man's hand tomorrow, how can he

Be suffered to die before necessity
Is through with him? No, you are, and he is,
Held for the moment in the will of heaven,
And neither one may act until the time.

SAUL

Suppose, Commander, that I killed you now?
Not, mind you, only for my own revenge,
But for the shattering of fate, in hope
To overthrow and break the will of heaven?
And, Minister, for your part, are you sure
The same divine will is protecting you?

MINISTER

No, master, killing me will alter nothing.
Yet there is one more thing, I'm sorry to say.
For David will accept the crown from you,
Then order your immediate death—and why?
Because you shed the sacred blood of Saul.

COMMANDER (*sits down*)

My death? My lord, what have I done to you?

SAUL

Why have you told us these things? You must know
Tale-bearers, never high in favor, are
Least so when all they have to tell is ill.

MINISTER

Duty forbids my holding back. Besides,
It was the woman's fault. She showed me all.

THE WITCH

O sir, do not believe him. It was he
Who begged me for a vision of his own.
He hoped to see the image of himself,
He said, deserting to the Philistine.

SAUL

Oh so? And did he see this heart's desire?

MINISTER

No, no, my lord. That was only a joke,
A momentary thought such as crosses the mind
Of a contemptible poor creature like myself.
The destinies within the flames were silent
Concerning me. I do not matter there.
My lord, I am contemptible, I admit it.
But do not kill me.

SAUL

Why should I spare you or the woman? She
With damnable art, you with damnable malice,
Compound together to destroy my courage.
It's treason, I believe neither of you.
Could you not leave the image of a king
To stand holy and high before his trial?

COMMANDER

You're right, my lord. These are subversive acts.
Let them confess and die as they deserve.

MINISTER (*kneeling*)

Great king, I will confess myself a man
Minded to envy and malice, one of those
Who in his heart believes the world to be
A cynical joke, or else an accident
Hung emptily between the sun and moon
That fools may scratch their heads until they die
Doubting, believing, while it answers nothing.
And I confess it was envy and malice
That made me speak, though the woman warned against.
My sort of man will always want to see

The holy and high mocked at and spat upon.
We'd shape life over in our clever image.
I am, also, a coward—

COMMANDER

We'd make a man out of you, in the army.
But now it seems there will be no more army.

SAUL

Your reasoning is bringing you close to death.
I trusted you, Minister, for many years.
And now—

MINISTER

My wits are not enough to save my life?
But let me speak.

SAUL (*turning away for a moment*)
                    It wearies me, all this.
I was forgetting that nothing matters. Speak.

MINISTER

O no, great sir, believe
That for yourself, and not for me, the world
Grows great with the beauty of holiness,
Completes itself in a majestic meaning,
Though full of terror. What we knew tonight
Declares God's mystery behind the world,
Dividing the waters of time to show your passage.
Declares that earthly triumph and defeat
Fall short of the end—
                    O Saul, because you cared
Even in loneliness and pride, the Lord
Rebukes you but to take you to himself,
And punishes only as the father does

His child, in order to forgive. While I,
Because I did not care, have been forever
Excluded from the story of His will,
Which some men play in, while the others watch.

SAUL

Well said. But you will live, and I shall die.

MINISTER

I do not doubt that if it pleases you
You may destroy me now. Perhaps you will,
Because some cruelty has always been
Deep in your nature; cruelty and sorrow
Together made you turn against David.
But if you say it was the will of heaven
That made you as you are, may I not say
The same will made me trivial and clever,
Both of us members of one mystery?
We cowards have our kind of courage, King;
It never lets us keep our mouths shut.

COMMANDER

I have a better way, if the king will permit.

SAUL

What does it matter to me? Either all men,
Or some men, or none at all, are subject
To God's wisdom and love that move the world.
He may say I was cruel to David, and
It was for that I lost the kingdom; then
He might say I was kind to Amalek
And lost the kingdom for my kindness; either
Or both become inscrutable toward the end.
Say what you like, Commander. The king permits.

COMMANDER
  Instead of slaying this civilian now,
  Though he deserves it, offer him the chance
  To take the field and fight with us today,
  And learn at least how men comport themselves
  In time of peril.

MINISTER
                    Can one forget so soon?
  But yes, agreed. I'll let you put a spear
  Into my hand, or whatever it is you use,
  And make my debut. I am curious to see
  How destiny accomplishes itself
  In spite of people.

COMMANDER
                    Under the circumstances,
  I am willing to forget the minister's
  Behavior. And if the king agrees,
  Let's drink to it.

SAUL
                    Let it be as you say.

                                    (*They drink.*)

  I am pleased to put my anger off. More wine.

THE WITCH (*pouring wine*)
  It is comforting to see you friends again.
  It often takes people that way, you know,
  People who come to me to see their future.
  They squabble among themselves and blame each other.
  It's all your fault, says one, and the other says,
  Had you acted otherwise than as you did—
  But there, I tell myself, is just the point:
  No one acts otherwise than as he does,

What might have been is hidden in what is;
That may be why the future is so harsh.
For as a general rule, I find, no one
Who doesn't fear the future wants to know it.
And yet it's strange, how quickly they forget.

MINISTER

Forget? How can they simply cancel out
What they compelled their senses to receive?

COMMANDER

This one more drink, and that will be plenty.
We shall have much hard work to do today,
A little moderate drinking before a fight,
In my experience, does no harm; one must
Know where to stop, however. My Lord the King.

(*He raises cup, drinks.*)
Now let us drink to courage.

(*They all drink.*)

MINISTER

No, it won't do. I'll drink to courage, but
I haven't got it, not that kind at least.
It's quite ridiculous. I try to see myself
Staggering around the field, waving a sword
And shouting. But I'm not that kind of creature.
Even this little bit of wine, and I
Begin to giggle at the thought. Great men,
The Lord made you the way you are, heroes,
For reasons of his own. He must have had
Some splendid reason, too, for making me
A clever, comfortable fellow. I'll stay home.

COMMANDER

You're under orders now, my man. You'll march
Wherever the others march, and do as you're told.

MINISTER

I must obey.

(aside)

But I'll carry two shields and no spear.

SAUL (at table, eating)

Excellent roast. You are a rare good cook.

THE WITCH

One learns, my Lord, one learns. My husband, while
He lived, cared specially about good food.
And hospitality was his first rule.

(All eat; the scene slowly
begins to lighten.)

SAUL

You know, my dear, I could have been content
To live as you do here, far from the noise
Of kingdoms and the world's contentions.
I never wanted to be a king, you know,
But came to it only by accident.
I was a farm boy, and my father sent me
After some half a dozen mules that strayed.
I went to get advice of the old man of God,
A man named Samuel, which way I should go.
And this old man—strange as a dream it is,
Just to remember—set me in the place
Of honor at his table, and put before me
The shoulder of the roast, as you have done,
Next day, in the holy place of his house,
Anointed me with oil. I was a frightened

Young fellow in those days, I hid myself
Among the baggage when the tribes assembled,
Until they found me, brought me forth, and all
The people shouted and said God save the king. . . .
Gentlemen, I've come a long road since then.

COMMANDER

My Lord, the sky is starting to light up,
The night is over, we must hasten on.

SAUL

Yes, I mustn't sit reminiscing here
While great concerns are waiting on our presence.

MINISTER (*aside*)

Praise to the Lord, the Holy One of Israel,
Who with the morning brings renewal of illusion.

SAUL

I've just remembered an old song we sang
About a man named Lamech—
    If Cain shall be avenged sevenfold,
    Truly Lamech seventy and sevenfold—
That's how it goes. We sang it on the march.
The funny thing is, nobody ever knew
Who Lamech was, or what he did. And now
It reminds me how the women used to sing,
Dancing to music before the city gates—
    Saul hath slain his thousands
    And David his ten thousands.
It made me angry then, but now—no matter.
What's gone was sometimes happy, but it's gone.
And maybe I shall slay ten thousand yet.

Come, gentlemen.
And you, my dear, our thanks for what you've done.
You have been royally hospitable.

> (*He kisses the Witch
> affectionately.*)

THE WITCH

Farewell, King Saul. But there is one thing more;
It's customary for some small contribution,
A token payment. . . .

SAUL

Minister, pay this woman. Be generous,
But reasonable. We'll wait for you out there.

COMMANDER

And don't imagine you can stop behind.

> (*Saul and the Commander leave.*)

MINISTER (*giving money*)

They have forgotten! And they are going forth
As blind men, fateless. What was in the wine?

THE WITCH

How can you say so, sir? You drank the wine.
But in a sense, as it is written, they drink
The wine of the condemned in the house of their God.

MINISTER

It's true, I drank the wine, yet I remember.
The house of God, you mean, is everywhere
With those men who would have it so, while I
Must blunder through the battlefield with my
Absurd and heavy knowledge of the end.
Who would believe me? Knowing, and not believing,
A burden I must try to carry quietly.

(He goes out.)
(Saul and the Commander are heard singing
several times, their voices growing more
distant:
If Cain shall be avenged sevenfold
Truly Lamech seventy and sevenfold.*)*

THE WITCH

The fire dies in daylight now, and men
Wake from their dreams into the mercy of time.

V Cain

Cain

A field at the edge of a forest. Two altars, or fireplaces anyhow,
one blackened and smoking, the other clean stone. To the second
altar, enter Cain carrying vegetables.

CAIN

The corn is coming along,
Tomatoes ripening up nicely, in a week
There should be melons. The apples
Are still green, but, then, after what happened
It might be as well if apples were not mentioned.
There is a good deal I don't understand
About that story, often as I've heard it told.
Mother doesn't like to discuss it, of course,
And I suspect that Adam my father
Is not entirely clear himself as to what happened,
Though he wears a very wise expression.

(Enter Abel.)

ABEL

Well! My sacrifices accepted for the day, I see.
And nothing more to be done for the moment.
Not bad. But you, brother,
I don't see any flames at your offering.
It's blood and meat the Lord likes,
Charred on the outside, red and juicy inside;
There's something unmanly about vegetables,
I always say. That's probably your trouble.

CAIN

Go on, amuse yourself at my expense,
I guess you have the right, for certainly
God favors your offerings of meat,
And leaves my vegetables alone. He leaves
The flowers too, that I bring

Because they are lovely, a something extra
To ornament the altar, and do Him honor
—These lilies that are blooming now.

ABEL (*laughing*)

You can't imagine the mighty God of All
Eating a lily! What God wants
Is strength. Strong men want strong meat.

CAIN

If He made All, He made the lilies too.
And He can't be like a man.

ABEL

I'm not arguing, I'm telling you,
It's simply a matter of fact.
The Lord has put His blessing on blood and meat.
Therefore He prefers me before you,
And I prosper greatly, and sit on the hillside
Watching my flocks, while you
Sweat in your vegetable patch.

CAIN

You have to kill those poor little lambs.

ABEL

Well, it's a man's work anyhow.

CAIN

It's horrible. I've heard them bleat
Before you cut the throat, and I've seen
The fear dumb in their eyes. What must it be like,
I wonder, to die?

ABEL

We can't tell, till one of us does.
I expect you'll be the first.

CAIN

Me? Why me?

ABEL

It's perfectly simple. Death is a punishment.
In dying we are punished for our sin.

CAIN

Our sin? I haven't sinned. What have I done?

ABEL

We have all sinned, and all will die.
But God's not respecting your offerings
Is a sign that you will be the first.

CAIN

You sound rather pleased about it.

ABEL

Do you suppose I want to be the first?
No, I am essentially a conservative person.
And I can see, looking at my lambs,
That dying's a grim business. I'm in no hurry.
It's only fit that you go first—you were born first.
Vegetarian!

CAIN

I don't understand. What have I done
That was wrong, or you that was right?
Father and Mother began the fault,
I know the story as well as you do.

ABEL

You don't accept life as it is, that's your trouble.
Things are the way they are, that's all.
They've been that way from the beginning.

CAIN

Which isn't so very long ago.

ABEL

And they will always be as they are.
Accept it, Cain. Face up to reality.

CAIN

That's easy for a winner to say.

(*Enter Adam and Eve.*)

CAIN and ABEL

Father! Mother!

(*They bow their heads.*)

ADAM

That's right, respect. It's a proper respect
As from the children to the parents
That keeps the world going round. It's a fine day,
And life is what you make it, isn't that so?
And both boys working hard, yes, that's right.
"In the sweat of thy face shalt thou eat thy bread"
Is what He said to me, but it's not so bad
When the children sweat for the father's bread.

(*He picks a tomato from Cain's
altar and eats it.*)

CAIN

Father, that is my offering to the Lord.

ADAM

Don't worry, I won't eat it all. Anyhow,
The Lord seems to prefer the flesh and fat
That Abel provides. I must say
That I agree. I'm eating this
Only to stave off hunger till mealtime.
Abel, I smell roast lamb. Good!

ABEL

Yes, the Lord God has received the essence,
And we may eat whatever is left over.

CAIN

It seems to me that everything is left except the smoke.

ABEL

Don't talk of what you don't understand.

ADAM

It is obvious, Cain, that you don't know
The first principle of sacrifice. It is
The divine effluvium of the beast that rises
To God in heaven, and does Him honor.
A spiritual essence Himself, He feeds on spirit.
The grosser parts are the leftovers of His meal,
Which we may eat, if we do so with humble hearts.

EVE

Why doesn't He eat the divine effluvium
Of Cain's vegetables?

ABEL

Whoever heard
Of burning vegetables? Our God
Is an eater of meat, meat, meat.

ADAM

Mother, don't mix in the relations of man with God.
Remember what happened last time.

(*There is a silence.*)

EVE

It wasn't my fault. It was only a mistake.

ADAM

A mistake to end all mistakes.

EVE

You listened to me, wise as you are.

ADAM

It proves the wisdom of my not doing so again.
He for God alone, and she for God in him;
Remember that, and there won't be any trouble.

CAIN

Sir, what really did happen last time,
I mean in the Garden?

ABEL

What's past is past. Cain still believes
There's something that he doesn't understand,
Or that you haven't told us, which would make
Some difference to his situation.

EVE (*to Cain*)

My poor boy, my poor, dear boy, I too
Go over it and over it in my mind, I too,
Though what I did is said to be so dreadful,
Feel that the Lord's way with me
Was very arbitrary, to say the least.

ADAM

Woman, enough. You'll make us more trouble.

ABEL

And as for Cain, he should have the tact
Not to pursue a subject which so evidently
Causes his mother pain.

(*to Cain*)

Also, our food is ready.
You may do as you please about that slop of yours,
But *this family* is going to eat.

(*Cain sits to one side, the rest to the other. Cain starts
eating a tomato.*)

ADAM

　Not, however, before properly rendering thanks
　To the Most High. Cain, have the decency
　To control your appetite until Abel
　Has sanctified our meal with prayer. Abel.

ABEL

　Permit us, O Lord, this tender beast
　Slain in Thy Holy Name, Amen.

(*All eat.*)

ADAM

　Mm, good.

CAIN

　Won't you let me have some? It smells good,
　And I would give you all this fruit.

ADAM

　Dear boy, don't let us go all over this again.
　It's not that we don't care for you personally,
　But we simply cannot afford to offend the Lord.
　If He does not respect your offering, Cain,
　It would be presumptuous in us to do so.
　If He means to separate you by this sign,
　We must not disobey.

ABEL

　To each according to his labor, you know.

CAIN

　But I haven't done anything wrong—
　As far as I'm aware, that is.

ADAM

　As far as you're aware, or we. Who knows
　The hidden meaning of God's mysteries?
　By the sign you are set off, and that's enough.

ABEL

    I'd set him further off. Suppose that God
    In His displeasure should strike Cain
    With fire from Heaven? I know that God
    Can do whatever He will, but still
    If we sit this close there might just be an accident.

CAIN (*moving a bit further away*)

    I don't want to be a danger to you, you all
    Seem to understand things so much better than I do.
    But what have I done wrong? Answer me that.

ADAM

    Ah, as to that, you would have to ask Him.

                               (*He points upward.*)

CAIN

    Did He really speak to you, Himself—then?

ADAM

    He did indeed, yes. Your father has spoken with God.

CAIN

    What does He look like?

ADAM

    Oh, you don't really see Him, you know,
    He doesn't have a form. There was a Voice.

EVE (*covering her ears*)

    Don't. Don't remind me. That Voice!

ADAM

    Mother, have more respect. We are talking
    Of divine things. Besides, who was responsible
    For His talking to us in that voice,
    And saying what He said? Remember that,
    Consider your sin, be quiet.

ABEL

    Cain thinks, because he is a gardener,
    That he would have been at home in a Garden.
    It's illogical, Cain, to suppose
    The Garden of the Lord would be anything like yours.

CAIN

    Illogical, yes. Yet if I reason it out,
    It does appear that God did once favor gardens,
    Since, after all, He put our parents there.
    And if I ask myself why He has turned against
    Garden and gardener, I will have to answer
    That what our parents did while they were there
    Was the thing that changed His mind.

ADAM

    I will not have blasphemy, Cain,
    And particularly not while we are at meat.
    As for disrespect for your father,
    I will not have that at any time. After all,
    Your mother went through much suffering
    To bring you into the world, while I
    Labored to give you food and all good things.
    For you to reward us with ingratitude
    Proves, to my mind, a hidden fault in you,
    And sufficiently explains why the All-Wise
    Does not respect your offerings as Abel's;
    Some wickedness, my boy, which is bringing you to sin.

EVE

    But truly, father, it was our fault.
    It was my fault first, then it was yours.

ADAM

    We may have made an error of judgment.
    Does Cain suppose he could have done better?

We tried our best to give you boys
A decent life and bring you up to be honest,
Industrious, pleasing in the sight of the Lord.
As a matter of fact, I am convinced
It was a piece of luck to have got out of that garden.
It was no place to bring up children in.
You would have had everything provided for you,
No need to learn the manly virtues,
The dignity of toil, the courage of independence.
No, Cain, hard work never hurt anybody.
What happened to us was the will of God,
Which shows He did not mean us to sit around
On our behinds in a garden all our lives,
But to get out in the world and become
The masters of it.

ABEL

                                Inventors of the knife,
    The wheel, the bow.

ADAM

    Sometimes I could bless that serpent!

EVE

    Stop! What dreadful things you are saying.
    Shame, labor, and the pains of birth
    The woman knows. Those are the fruits
    That grew on the forbidden tree, and I,
    The first to sin, was the first to know them.
    I shall be the first to know death also.

ADAM

    Mother, don't excite yourself. What's done is done.
    As for death, no need to talk of that, I hope,
    For many years.

ABEL

The little lambs are peaceful after death,
Mother. There's only a moment of fright,
And then it's over.

CAIN

But there's that moment, that small moment.
A man might do anything, if he thought enough
How there's no way out but through that moment.
He might become wild, and run away,
Knowing there was nowhere to run, he might . . .

ABEL

Might what?

CAIN

Kill.

ABEL

He might leave off babbling in that manner,
And remember he is a man, if not a very good one.

CAIN

But if a man, even if not a very good one,
Is turned away by his God, what does he do?
Where does he go? What could he do
Worse than what is already done to him?
For there is God on the one hand,
And all the world on the other, and this man
Between them. Why should he care,
Seeing he cannot save himself?

ADAM

These are dangerous thoughts, Cain.
That man might better think
Wherein he has offended.

*(The sky darkens. Thunder is heard, and
lightning seen.)*

ABEL

Aha! he's done it now, with his talk.
Did you think He would not have heard?
Did you consider the rest of us?

CAIN

I only meant to ask.

ABEL

You are being answered.

(He points to the sky.)

ADAM

I am afraid, Cain, that Abel is right.
I have faced up to God one time in my life,
It was enough. The coming storm
You brought down on yourself, and you must face
The consequences. I am sorry for you.
Eve, come. Come, Abel. We shall seek shelter elsewhere.

*(They leave, and Cain stands alone. Lightning
flashes, sounds of thunder, then a stillness.)*

CAIN

Ah, they are right. I am going to die,
And I deserve to die. As Abel said,
There is no argument, the uneasy fear
I feel in my stomach tells me I am wrong,
Am guilty of everything, everything,
Though I cannot say what it is. Lord!
Lord God! Master! I am a wicked man,
The thoughts of my heart are wicked
And I don't know why. Punish me, Lord,
Punish me, but do not let me die.

(Cain kneels.)

THE VOICE OF GOD in the silence
   Cain.

        Cain.

                Cain.

CAIN
   Here I am.

GOD
   What do you want?

CAIN
   I want to know.

GOD
   Ask.

CAIN
   Why do You respect my brother's offerings and not mine?

GOD
   That is not the question you want to ask.

CAIN
   Why do You prefer Abel to me?

GOD
   That again is not it. You must ask to the end.

                                  (*A long silence.*)

CAIN
   Why are things as they are?

GOD
   I will debate it with you. Do you know
   That things are as they are?

CAIN
   But—but they *are*, they just *are*. Besides,
   My father says they are.

GOD

Cain, I am your father.

CAIN

Sir, as you say.

GOD

Do you want things to be other than as they are?

CAIN

I want my offering to be acceptable, Sir.
I want my offering to be preferred over Abel's.
I want to be respected, even as he is now.

GOD

Why do you trouble yourself about it, then?
The thing is easy. If you do well,
Will you not be accepted? And if you do not do well,
Look, sin lies at the door.

CAIN

Sir, I do not understand.

GOD

Cain, Cain, I am trying to tell you.
All things can be done, you must only
Do what you will. Things are as they are
Until you decide to change them,
But do not be surprised if afterward
Things are as they are again. What is to stop you
From ruling over Abel?

(*again, after a silence*)

CAIN

I do not know.

(*Thunder.*)

I do not know. I said I do not know.
He is not there and I am alone.

(*The sky clears, the light grows stronger.*)

And this is Abel's knife, which he left here
In his hurry to escape the storm he hoped would slay me.
And that storm was God.
And this is the knife which cuts the throats
Of acceptable sacrifices.

(*Enter Abel.*)

ABEL

You're still alive. Surely the ways of the Lord
Are past understanding. Have you seen my knife?

CAIN (*still kneeling*)

I have it here.

ABEL

Throw it to me then. I'm still uneasy
About coming close to you.

CAIN

I have spoken with God, Abel. If you want your knife,
Come over here and have it. God said things,
Abel, such as I never heard from you. He told me
About the will. Do what you will, He said.
And more than that, He said: You must
Do what you will. Abel, do you understand
That saying?

ABEL (*approaching*)

The knife, I want the knife.

CAIN

Here, then.

(*He rises, stabbing Abel, who falls.*)

My sacrifices shall be acceptable.

ABEL

My God, what have you done?

(*He dies.*)

CAIN (*standing over him*)

I have done what I willed. I have changed
The way things are, and the first man's death is done.
It was not much, I have seen some of his lambs
Die harder.

GOD (*speaking casually, conversationally, without thunder*)

Do you find it good, what you've done? Or bad?

CAIN (*as though talking to himself*)

Good? Bad? It was my will that I did.
I do not know anything of good or bad.

GOD

Do you find that you have changed
Things as they are?

CAIN (*staring at Abel*)

There is this difference, certainly.
And I have changed inside myself. I see now
That a man may be the master here.

GOD

Like that man on the ground?

CAIN

A man. Myself.

GOD

How peaceful he is, lying there.

CAIN

That's true, I feel uneasy, myself.
Abel, what have you to say to me now?
Well, speak up.

GOD

He will not speak.

CAIN

He is very quiet now, considering
How much he used to talk. How lonely
Everything has become! Mother! Father!   (*He shouts.*)

GOD

They will do to you as you have done to him.

CAIN

Then I must run away.

GOD

Where will you run?

CAIN

Anywhere, to be alone.
There are no other people.

GOD

You're wrong about that. Everywhere
Men are beginning, and everywhere they believe
Themselves to be alone, and everywhere
They are making the discovery of the conditions
Under which they are as they are. One of these
Discoveries has just been made, by you.
You will be alone, but alone among many,
Alone in every crowd.

CAIN

Seeing me set apart, they will kill me.

GOD

They would. But I have set my sign
Upon your forehead, that recognizing you,
Men will be afeared. Shunning you, scorning you,
Blaming you, they may not kill you.

CAIN (*kneeling*)

Lord God! You spoke, and I did not know.

GOD

I send you away, Cain. You are one
Of my holy ones, discoverer of limits,
Your name is the name of one of the ways,
And you must bear it. You must bear
The everlasting fear no one can stop,
The everlasting life you do not want,
The smell of blood forever on your hand.
You are the discoverer of power, and you
Shall be honored among men that curse you,
And honored even in the moment of the curse.
From your discovery shall proceed
Great cities of men, and well defended,
And these men, your descendants, shall make
Weapons of war, and instruments of music,
Being drawn thereto by the nature of power;
But they will not be happy, and they will not know
Peace or any release from fear.

CAIN

May I not die?

GOD

Because of My sign, only you
May destroy yourself. And because of your fear,
You won't. For you have found
An idea of Me somewhat dangerous to consider,
And mankind will, I believe, honor your name
As one who has faced things as they are,
And changed them, and found them still the same.

CAIN

If I were sorry, would you raise Abel up?

GOD

No.

CAIN

Then I am not sorry. Because You have saved me
From everything but the necessity of being me,
I say it is Your fault. None of this need have happened.
And even my mother's temptation by the serpent in the Gar-
den
Would not have happened but for You; I see now,
Having chosen myself, what her choice must have been.

GOD

Cain, I will tell you a secret.

CAIN

I am listening.

GOD

I was the serpent in the Garden.

CAIN

I can believe that, but nobody else will.
I see it so well, that You are the master of the will
That works two ways at once, whose action
Is its own punishment, the cause
That is its own result. It will be pain to me
To reject You, but I do it, in Your own world,
Where everything that is will speak of You,
And I will be deaf.

GOD

You do not reject Me. You cannot.

CAIN

I do not expect it to be easy.

(after a silence)

I said: I do not expect it to be easy.
But He is gone, I feel His absence.
As, after the storm's black accent,
The light grows wide and distant again,
So He is gone. Of all He said to me,
Only one thing remains. I send you away,
He said: Cain, I send you away.
But where is *Away?* Is it where Abel is,
My brother, as lonely and still as that?

> (*Enter Adam and Eve; Cain turns away his face.*)

ADAM (*at a distance*)
Was it the thunder, Abel, the lightning?

> (*Coming closer, he sees that Abel is on the ground.*)

It can't be. There has been a mistake.

EVE
Abel, my son, my lamb.

> (*She runs to the corpse and throws herself down.*)

ADAM
Monster! Unnatural child! Did you do this?
Lord God, let it not go unpunished,
Let it be swiftly visited.

CAIN (*still turned away*)
Suppose it was God that struck Abel down?
Cannot the Lord do as He will do?

ADAM
Liar! I will never believe it, never.

CAIN
Well, then, it was a lie. I did it.
But had it been the other way, and I

The brother lying there, would you not have said,
As I have heard you say so many times,
What the Lord does is well done?

ADAM

Vicious boy! Have you not done enough?
Would you go on to stand against your father?

EVE

Leave off, leave off. One son and the other son,
All that I had, all that I cared to have,
One son and the other son, and from the beginning
This was the end I carried, the end we lay together
Taking our pleasure for, is now accomplished.

CAIN

I stand, it seems, alone. Neither against
Nor for father or mother or anything.

ADAM

If the Lord God will not punish, I must.

EVE

Leave off, leave off. All that we had
Is halved, and you would destroy the other half?
Abel my son and Cain my son. Old man,
It is your seed that from the beginning
Was set at odds. You ate the fruit
Of the tree of knowledge as well as I,
And sickened of it as well as I, and swelled with lust
As I swelled with the fruit of lust,
And have you yet no knowledge?

ADAM

Woman, be quiet. This is not woman's work.

EVE

    Oh, fool, what else if not woman's work?
    The fruit of the curse has ripened till it fell,
    Can you refuse to swallow it? But you will swallow it,
    I tell you, stone and all, one son and the other son.

ADAM

    Cain, I am an old man, but it comes to me
    That I must do to you as you did to your brother.

EVE

    Fooled in the Garden, and fooled out of it!

CAIN (*turning his face to Adam, who falls back*)

    Sir, you will do nothing. I am young and strong,
    And I have the knife—but no, that's not it,
    I do not want to stand against you, but I must.

ADAM

    There is a sign, a wound, there on your brow
    Between the eyes. Cain, I am afraid of you.
    There is a terror written on your face.

CAIN

    And I am afraid of you. That is my fear
    You see written upon me, that your fear answers to.
    I am forbidden to be sorry for what I did,
    Forbidden to pity you, forbidden to kiss
    My mother's tears, and everywhere
    In everything forbidden. I feel myself filled
    With this enormous power that I do not want,
    This force that tells me I am to go,
    To go on, always to go on, to go away
    And see you both, and this place, never again.

EVE

    My son, my only one, you won't go away?
    I'll face the fear I see upon your face,
    And you'll comfort me for what you did to me.

ADAM

    And stay me in my age? Cain, I accept it,
    Though I shall never understand it, this
    That you have done, this final thing
    In a world where nothing seemed to end,
    Is somehow the Lord God's doing. I fear you,
    My son, but I will learn to still my fear,
    If you will stay.

CAIN

    No. I would change things if I could.
    I tried to change things once, and the change
    Is as you see; we cannot change things back,
    Which may be the only change worth having,
    So the future must be full of fear, which I
    Would spare you. If this is riddling talk,
    Let it go by; or, to speak plainly,
    I am afraid my fear would make me kill you
    If I stayed here.

EVE

                This is the end
    That we began with. Why should we not
    Curse God and die?

ADAM

    Woman, be careful.

EVE

    I have been careful, full of care.
    My son, my darling, why not kill us both?

141

It would be only what we did to you;
And that was only what was done to us.

CAIN

Mother, Mother, I must not hear you.
You and I, we understand things alike,
And that is curse enough, maybe. But he
May have his own curse, which we
Don't understand, that is, to go on,
Into the darkness, into the light,
Having the courage not to know
That what I do to him is what he does to me,
And both of us compelled, or maybe
It is a blessing, the blindness of too much light
That comes from staring at the sun.
                                        Father,
I'd bless you if I could, but I suspect
That God believes in you.
And now farewell,
If that is possible; try not to remember me.

                    (*Cain goes. The scene begins to darken.*)

ADAM

Old woman, we are alone again, and the night
Beginning to come down. Do you remember
The first night outside the Garden?

EVE

We slept in the cold sparkle of the angel's sword,
Having cried ourselves asleep.

ADAM

If we went back, do you think, and stood
At the gate, and said plainly, kill us
Or take us back, do you think . . . ?

EVE

No.

ADAM

You're right, we couldn't any more go back
Than you could be my rib again, in my first sleep.
The water in the rivers running out of Eden,
Where must that water be now, do you think?

EVE

It must be elsewhere, somewhere in the world;
And yet I know those rivers glitter with water still.
Abel my son and my son Cain, all that we had is gone.
Old as we are, we come to the beginning again.

ADAM

Doing as we would, and doing as we must. . . .
The darkness is so lonely, lonelier now
Than on the first night, even, out of Eden.
Having what we've had, and knowing what we know. . . .

EVE

What have we had, and what do we know?
The years are flickering as a dream, in which
Our sons are grown and gone away. Husband,
Take courage, come to my arms, husband and lord.
It is the beginning of everything.

ADAM

Must we take the terrible night into ourselves
And make the morning of it? Again?
Old woman, girl, bride of the first sleep,
In pleasure and in bitterness all ways
I love you till it come death or daylight.